VIENNA

GUIDES

Welcome to Vienna!

This opening fold-out contair   ..s of valuable information, handy
tips and useful addresses, and a general map of Vienna to help you visualize
the six districts discussed in this guide. On the map, indicated by a star, are
the ten sights not to be missed if your visit is a short one.

Discover Vienna through six districts and six maps

A Stephansdom / Graben
B Freyung / Hofburg
C Ring / Josefstadt / Alsergrund
D Leopoldstadt / Prater
E Karlplatz / Wienzeile / Belvedere
F Schönbrunn / Hietzing

For each district there is a double-page of addresses (restaurants – listed in
ascending order of price – cafés, bars, tearooms, music venues, and stores),
followed by a fold-out map for the relevant area with the essential places to
see (indicated on the map by a star ★). These places are by no means all that
Vienna has to offer, but to us they are unmissable. The grid-referencing
system (**A** B2) makes it easy for you to pinpoint addresses quickly on the map.

Transportation and hotels in Vienna

The last fold-out consists of a transportation map and four pages of practical
information that include a selection of hotels.

Index

Lists all the street names, sites, and monuments featured in this guide.

KEY DATES

SECESSION STYLE

ARCHITECTURE

Baroque The Habsburgs turned Vienna into a great baroque city during the Counter Reformation. This style is epitomized by the **Karlskirche** (**E** D1).
Primitive baroque (17th c.) Churches and palaces built by Italian architects; **Jesuitenkirche** (**A** C3), **Theresianum** (**E** D2).
Austrian baroque The most beautiful 18th-c. baroque buildings were designed by two great national architects, J. B. Fischer von Erlach and J. L. von Hildebrandt; **Kinsky** (**B** B2) and **Trautson** (**C** C5) palaces.
Jugendstil & Secession The beginning of the 20th century saw the birth of German Art Nouveau (Jugendstil) and Art Deco (Secession) trends. For Jugendstil and its curving lines, see **Karlsplatz subway station** (**E** D1). For the Secession style and its geometric lines see the **Secession Building** (**E** C1).
Modern Vienna Built under the Austro-marxist administration, the period known as 'Red Vienna' (1919–34). **Karl-Marx-Hof** (subway: Heiligenstadt); 1,382 public housing apartments designed by Karl Ehn in 1927.
Contemporary Vienna Designs by renowned architects (Hermann Czech, Friedensreich Hundertwasser, Robert Krier, Hans Hollein); **Hundertwasserhaus** (**D** D4).

November
Wien Modern
→ *Throughout Nov; wienmodern.at*
Contemporary music at the Konzerthaus (**A** D6) and at the Musikverein (**E** D1).
December
The Emperor's Ball
→ *Dec 31*
At the Hofburg (**B** C4).

BUDGET

The cost of living is quite high in Vienna.
Note that credit cards are not accepted everywhere.
Accommodation
A room in the city center: €80–90.
Eating out
For a main course and a dessert, excluding drinks, allow €10–25, plus ten percent for a tip.
Out and about
A beer: €2.30; a *Melange*: €3; entrance to a nightclub: €7.

Museums
Entry fee: €8–10. Municipal museums are free the first Sunday of every month (except Mozarthaus Vienna, **A** C3).

OPENING TIMES

Meals
→ *Food is generally available throughout the day (noon–10pm); dinner is around 7pm*
Banks
→ *Usually Mon-Fri 8am–3pm (5.30pm Thu)*
Going out
→ *Bars close at 1am, clubs around 4am but some are open until dawn*
→ *Opera, concerts and theater shows start at 7.30pm*
Museums
→ *They are closed Mon or Tue, Dec 24-26 and Dec 31-Jan 1. Late opening Thu or Fri evenings*
Shops
→ *Mon-Sat 10am–7pm (6pm Sat)*

Mail
Hauptpost (**A** D2)
→ *Fleischmarkt 19; Daily 7am (9am Sat-Sun)– 10pm*
Central post office.

EATING OUT

Where?
Beisl: a bistro.
Gasthaus: an inn serving family-type meals.
Heuriger: a wine tavern.
Imbiss: for fast food and snacks.
Keller: a tavern.
Lokal: a bar.
Würstelstand: a sausage stall.
Some Austrian and Viennese specialties
Apfelstrudel: an apple turnover with raisins.
Frankfurter mit Senf: Frankfurter sausages with mustard.
Frittatensuppe: a clear beef broth with thin strips of pancake.
Leberknödel: liver

CITY PROFILE

- Capital city of the Republic of Austria, and one of its nine states (Land) ▪ 160 sq. miles ▪ 23 boroughs ▪ 1.7 million inh. ▪ 30 percent of the national wealth
- Fairly dry and cold winters (0C/32F); mild and humid summers (20–25C/ 68–77F)
- *Dialekt*: Viennese slang

LANDMARKS

- The Ring, former 16th-century ramparts
- The Gürtel, outer ring
- The Donaukanal
- The Danube

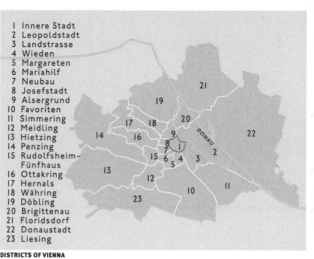

1 Innere Stadt
2 Leopoldstadt
3 Landstrasse
4 Wieden
5 Margareten
6 Mariahilf
7 Neubau
8 Josefstadt
9 Alsergrund
10 Favoriten
11 Simmering
12 Meidling
13 Hietzing
14 Penzing
15 Rudolfsheim–Fünfhaus
16 Ottakring
17 Hernals
18 Währing
19 Döbling
20 Brigittenau
21 Floridsdorf
22 Donaustadt
23 Liesing

DISTRICTS OF VIENNA

WWW

→ *austria.info*
Comprehensive site of the Austrian National Tourist Office.
→ *wien.info*
All the city's events.
Internet cafés
Speednet Café (A B1)
→ *Morzinplatz 4*
Tel. 532 57 50; Daily 8am (10am Sat-Sun)–midnight
Generous time slots and the best rates.
Cafés with free Wi-Fi
→ *freewave.at/hotspots*

TOURIST INFO

Tourist-Info Wien (A A5)
→ *Albertinaplatz*
Tel. 24 555
Daily 9am–7pm; wien.info
The tourist office – hotel bookings, stamps, sale of opera, concerts, theater tickets, train tickets, etc. also at the airport arrival hall (daily 6am– 11pm).

Urlaubsservice Center
→ *Tel. 0810 10 18 18*
National Tourist Office, telephone service only.

TELEPHONE

UK / USA to Vienna
→ *00 (from the UK) / 011 (from the USA) + 43 (Austria) + 1 (Vienna) + number*
Within Austria
→ *0 + local code (1 for Vienna) + number*
Vienna to UK / USA
→ *00 + 44 (UK) / 1 (USA) + number (minus the 0 for the UK)*
Emergency numbers
Police
→ *Tel. 133*
Emergencies
→ *Tel. 144*
Fire service
→ *Tel. 122*

DIARY OF EVENTS

Public holidays
→ *Jan 1; Jan 6 (Epiphany);*
Easter Monday; May 1; Ascension Day; Whit Monday; June 15 (holy day); Aug 15; Oct 26 (national holiday); All Saints' Day; Dec 8 (Immaculate Conception); Dec 25–26.
January-February
New Year's Concert
→ *Jan 1*
At the Musikverein (**E** D1).
State Opera Ball
→ *Thu before Ash Wed*
April
Vinova
→ *First or second week; vinova.at*
Big wine festival at the Messezentrum (**D** F3).
Vienna Marathon
→ *End of the month; vienna-marathon.com*
From Reichsbrücke to Heldenplatz (**B** B4).
May-June
Wiener Festwochen
→ *Mid-May–mid-June; festwochen.at*
Theater, opera and dance.

Lange Nacht der Musik
→ *One evening in June*
Live music throughout the city.
Donauinselfest
→ *End of June; donauinselfest.at*
Concerts, sporting events, cabaret.
July-August
Jazz Fest Wien
→ *End June-mid-July; viennajazz.org*
Concerts at the Rathaus (**C** C4) and the Staatsoper (**B** D6).
Musikfilmfest
→ *July-Aug*
Outdoor movie screen opposite the Rathaus.
ImPulsTanz
→ *July-Aug; impulstanz.com*
Dance festival in various theaters.
October
Viennale
→ *End Oct; viennale.at*
The Vienna Film Festival.

Welcome to Vienna!

A Stephansdom / Graben
B Freyung / Hofburg
C Ring / Josefstadt / Alsergrund

D Leopoldstadt / Prater
E Karlsplatz / Wienzeile / Belvedere
F Schönbrunn / Hietzing

HERNALS

OTTAKRING

JOSEFSTADT

HERNALSER HAUPTSTRASSE

SANDLEITEN GASSE

GERSTHOFER

PETER-JORDAN-STR.

STRASSE

WÄHRINGER GÜRTEL

HERNALSER GÜRTEL

ALSER

NEUBAU GÜRTEL

MAROLTINGER GASSE

FLÖTZERSTEIG

GABLENZGASSE

WESTBAHNHOF

RUDOLFSHEIM

MARIAHILFER

MARIAHILFER STRASSE

MARIAHILFER GÜRTEL

AMEISGASSE

HADIKGASSE

HADIKGASSE

HIETZINGER KAI

SCHÖNBRUNNER

LINKE WIENZEILE

SCHÖNBRUNNER

Am Platz

SCHLOSS- STRASSE

★ **SCHLOSS SCHÖNBRUNN**

HIETZING

SCHLOSSPARK SCHÖNBRUNN

FRIEDHOF HIETZING

GRÜNBERGSTR.

MEIDLING

EICHENSTRASSE

FRIEDHOF MEIDLING

ALTMANNSDORFER

WIENERBERGSTRASSE

F

SCHLOSS HETZENDORF

BREITENFURTER STR.

GOLF- PLATZ

BRIGITTENAU

KONGRESS-ZENTRUM

WAGRAMER STR.

DONAU

KAISERMÜHLEN

HANDELSKAI

DRESDNER STRASSE

SPITTELAUER LÄNDE

BRIGITTENAUER LÄNDE

FRANZ-JOSEFS-BAHNHOF

PALAIS LIECHTENSTEIN

WÄHRINGER STRASSE

AUGARTEN

Gauss-Platz

ROSSAUER LÄNDE

OBERE DONAUSTRASSE

FRANZ-JOSEFS-KAI

FRACHTENBF. NORDWESTBF.

NORDBAHN STRASSE

LASSALLESTRASSE

Praterstern

A22

HANDELSKAI

DONAU

LANDESGERICHTSSTR.

STR.

TH. THERESIEN-STRASSE

JOSEFS-KAI

Julius-Raab-Platz

PRATERSTR.

UNTERE DONAU-STR.

WEISSGERBER LÄNDE

SCHÜTTEL-

LEOPOLDSTADT

PRATER

STADION

PRATER

B

A

GRABEN

★ ★ STEPHANSDOM

HOFBURG ★

VOLKS-GARTEN

NEUE BURG

★ STAATSOPER

STADT-PARK

Am Heumarkt

★ HUNDERTWASSERHAUS

ERDBERGER LÄNDE

D

MUSEUMS-QUARTIER

STR.

C

★ SECESSION

Karlsplatz

★ KARLSKIRCHE

LANDSTRASSE

RENNWEG

A23

A4

A4

LINKE WIENZEILE

RECHTE WIENZEILE

WIENER

HAUPT STRASSE

FAVORITENSTRASSE

WIEDNER

BELVEDERE-GARTEN

★ BELVEDERE

LANDSTRASSER GÜRTEL

SCHLACHTHAUSG.

RENNWEG

MARGARETEN

GÜRTEL

WIEDNER

SÜDBAHNHOF

SCHWEIZER GARTEN

SONNWEND-GASSE

ST.-MARXER FRIEDHOF

SIMMERINGER

STR.

MARGARETEN

GÜRTEL

STRASSE

EVANG. FRIEDHOF

E

SIMMERING

FAVORITEN

TRIESTER

RAXSTRASSE

FAVORITENSTRASSE

GRENZACKER STR.

A23

Altes Landgut

0   500   1 000 m

1/50 000 - 1 cm = 500 m

EXCURSIONS

NATURE RESERVE
CEMETERY
VINEYARD

EXCURSIONS

Mon-Sat 9.30am-7pm
(8pm Thu; 6pm Sat)
The only hypermarket in
the city center, with all the
top international brands.

Flea market
Beyond Naschmarkt (E B1)
→ Wienzeile
Sat 6.30am-6pm
Antique and second-hand
dealers.

Kunst & Antiquitäten
Markt Am Hof (B D2)
→ March-Dec;
Fri-Sat 10am-8pm
Antiquarian books,
second-hand objects, and
arts and crafts.

Christmas markets
→ Mid-Nov-end Dec, daily
The whole town is invaded
by little wooden chalets
serving Weihnachtspunsch
(Christmas punch).

GREEN SPACES

Stadtpark (A D5)
The biggest park bordering
the Ring: meandering
avenues and a gilded
statue of Johann Strauss.

Volksgarten (B B3)
The first public park (1823):
charming fountains, rose
beds, and the temple of
Theseus.

Botanischer Garten
der Universität (E D5)
Botanical gardens
boasting 9,000 species.

Türkenschanzpark
→ Buses 37A and 40A
This former Turkish
military encampment is
now a quiet park in the
upper part of the city.

VIENNA
ANOTHER WAY

Aboard a vintage tram
→ Tel. 786 0303
May-Oct: Sat-Sun; Departs
from Karlsplatz (**E** D1)
See the major monuments
on the Ring onboard a
1929 tram.

By bicycle
Pedal Power (D D2)
→ Ausstellungsstrasse 3
Tel. 729 72 34
Guided tours May-Sep:
daily 9.45am, 2.15pm;
Bike rental March-Oct: 8am-
7pm; pedalpower.at
A great way to discover
Vienna's treasures. Ride on
your own or with a guide.

On the Danube
DDSG Blue Danube
→ Tel 588 80
April-Oct: daily departure
from Reichsbrücke (**D** E1)
or Schwedenplatz (**A** D2);
€15; ddsg-blue-danube.at
A boat trip along the
Danube.

VIENNESE WORDS

Grüss Gott ('God be
praised'): Hello
Yo: approval
Servus: informal greeting
Schlamperei: typical
Viennese indolence
Gemütlichkeit: coziness,
intimacy and comfort;
the art of living

EXCURSIONS

**The waters of the Old
Danube (Alte Donau)**
→ Kaisermühlen subway
A former backwater
of the great river.

Grosse Gänsehäufel
A bathing resort on an
island accessible via a
bridge. Popular beaches,
including a nudist area.

Kleines Gänsehäufel
Charming peninsula.

Krapfenwaldlbad
→ By bus 38A; Tel. 320 15
01; May-Sep: daily 9am-
7pm (8am Sat-Sun)
Municipal swimming
pool: three pools among
the trees of the park, with
a clear view over the city.

Wienerwald
The 'Viennese forest',
at the foothills of the
eastern Alps.

The Kahlenberg
→ By bus 38A
Unique panorama of
Vienna, from an altitude
of 1,588 feet.

Lainzer Tiergarten
→ Tram 60, then bus 60B
Fifty miles of footpaths
in an oak and beech
forest, home to Bighorn
sheep and deer.

The Viennese vineyard
Grinzing and Nussdorf
→ To Grinzing with tram 38;
to Nussdorf with tram D
Two ancient wine-
growing villages on the
vine-clad lower slopes
of the Kahlenberg.

Baden
→ To Badner Bahn (16 mi
southwest); departs from
Oper; journey time: one hr
The famous Biedermeier-
style thermal spa.

Kurpark
The spa: luxury casino,
Jugendstil theater and
beautiful rose garden.

HAUS DER MUSIK

CAFÉ EUROPA

CAFÉ CENTRAL

dumplings with parsley.
Mehlspeise: a cream cake, specialty of Vienna.
Wiener Melange: the Viennese latte.
Sachertorte: a chocolate cake with apricot-jam glazing.
Schlagobers: chantilly cream.
Tafelspitz: a boiled piece of beef from the rump of a young ox, served with vegetables.
Wiener Schnitzel: a veal (though today often pork) escalope in breadcrumbs.

GUIDED TOURS

Wiener Spaziergänge
→ *Tel. 489 96 74*
wienguide.at
Group and individual tours with the official City of Vienna guides.

Vienna Sightseeing Tours (**E** D2)
→ *Goldeggasse 29*
Tel. 712 46 830;
viennasightseeingtours.com
Tours in English (min. four people) from €36/person.
Hop-On Hop-Off
→ *one-hour/two-hour tours:*
€13/€16; one-day pass: €20
Shuttle buses leave from the Staatsoper (**B** D6), and pass by the major tourist sites.

Wien Karte
→ *Travelcard available from Tourist-Info Wien, museums, hotels and tobacconists; valid 72 hours; € 18.50*
Unlimited travel on public transportation, reduced entry fee to most of the city's museums and monuments, and discounts in some cafés and shops.

SHOWS

Programs
Falter and City
→ *Weekly, on sale every Fri*
Two cultural guides with movies, concerts, exhibitions programs; plus current affairs, recommendations etc.
Wienprogramm
→ *Free monthly; in hotels and at Tourist-Info Wien*
Full programs and times.
Bookings & discounts
Wien-Ticket
→ *Tel 58885; wien-ticket.at*
WienXtra-Jugendinfo (**B** B5)
→ *Babenbergstr. 1*
Tel. 1799; Mon-Sat noon–7pm; wienxtra.at
Youth information center: programs and tickets at a reduced rate.
Balls
Wiener Fasching
→ *Dec 31-Shrove Tuesday; Wiener Ballkalender Brochure from Tourist-Info Wien*
The ball season opens with the Emperor's Ball, followed by that of the Opera and then the Philharmonic.
Opera houses
Staatsoper (**B** D6)
→ *Opernring 2*

Tel. 514 44 22 50
wiener-staatsoper.at
Daily performances in the original language.
Volksoper (**C** B1)
→ *Währinger Strasse 78*
Tel. 514 44 3670
volksoper.at
Popular operas in German.

SHOPPING

Department stores
Steffl (**A** B4)
→ *Kärntner Strasse 19*
Mon-Sat 9.30am–7pm
(8pm Thu-Fri; 6pm Sat)
Beauty products, fashion and accessories over three floors. Stylish and trendy.
Ringstrassen Galerien (**A** A6)
→ *Kärntner Ring 5–7*
Mon-Sat 10am–7pm
(6pm Sat)
Arcade with luxury stores.
Shopping mall
Kaufhaus Gerngross (**C** C6)
→ *Mariahilfer Strasse 42–48*
Tel. 521 800

KAPUZINERGRUFT

HAUS DER MUSIK

DOROTHEUM
KAPUZINER-KIRCHE
Neuer Markt
INNERE
PALAIS LOBKOWITZ
KAPUZINERGRUFT
SPIEGELGASSE
GLUCKG.
RAUHE
HIMMELPFORTGASSE
WINTERPALAIS DES PRINZ EUGEN
FÜHRICH-GASSE
AUGUSTINER-STRASSE
TEGETTHOFFSTR.
STR.
MALTESER-KIRCHE
SAVOYSCHES DAMENSTIFT
JOHANNES-
5
ALBERTINA
ST. ANNA
ANNAGASSE
MAYSEDERG.
KÄRNTNER
Albertinaplatz
HAUS DER MUSIK
KRUGERSTRASSE
SEILERSTÄTTE
OPERN-GASSE
PHILHARMO-NIKERSTR.
WALFISCHGASSE
STAATSOPER
KÄRNTNER STR.
SCHWARZENBERGSTRASSE
SCHELLING-
MAHLER-STRASSE
AKADEMIESTRASSE
KARLSPLATZ
U
Opern-passage
6
KÄRNTNER RING
0
100
200 m
A
B
Schwarzen platz

★ **Stephansdom** (**A** B3)
→ *Stephansplatz*
Tel. 515 52 35 26; Daily 6am (7am Sun) –10pm
In the heart of Vienna stands St Stephen's Cathedral, with its colorful ceramic tiled roof and its 390-foot spire. Enter through the imposing 13th-century Riesentor (Giants' Portal) and admire the countless polychromatic statues of angels, of saints and of the Church Fathers. The style is flamboyant Gothic, with ribbed vaults and an ornate pulpit (1515) by Anton Pilgram. The hand of the same master stone-carver is also evident in the self-portrait at the foot of the organ.

★ **Graben** (**A** A3)
The former Roman dike (Graben), and one of Vienna's most elegant thoroughfares, was pedestrianized in the 1970s. Tall bourgeois buildings house smart boutiques and neat rows of café terraces. In the center stands the giant votive column of the Plague, or Pestsäule (J.B.Fischer von Erlach, 1693), in classic baroque style: note the figure of the defeated Plague, an old witch struck down by an angel, and the statue of Leopold I praying.

★ **Peterskirche** (**A** A3)
→ *Petersplatz; Mon-Fri 7am–8pm; Sat-Sun 9am–9pm*
A huge grayish-green dome and a narrow façade that blends harmoniously into the surrounding square set back from the Graben. The magnificent St Peter's Church was built in 1733 by Montani and Hildebrandt. Its ornate baroque interior is a profusion of gilt, moldings and flourishes, and the oval dome is decorated with a wonderful fresco of the Assumption (1714) by Johann Michael Rottmayr.

★ **Kapuzinergruft** (**A** A5)
→ *Neuer Markt; Tel. 512 68 53*
Daily 10am–6pm
Beyond the austere entrance that leads to the stairs is a series of underground chambers t comprise the imperial bu vault. Founded in 1618, it contains the embalmed bodies of 145 members o the Habsburg dynasty. Th variety of tombs, includir that of Maria-Theresa (1717–80) is fascinating.

★ **Haus der Musik** (**A** B
→ *Seilerstätte 30; Tel. 513 4 50; Daily 10am–10pm*
The palace of Archduke K and former home of Otto Nicolai (1810–49), found of the prestigious Vienna Philharmonic orchestra.

STEPHANSDOM

GRABEN

PETERSKIRCHE

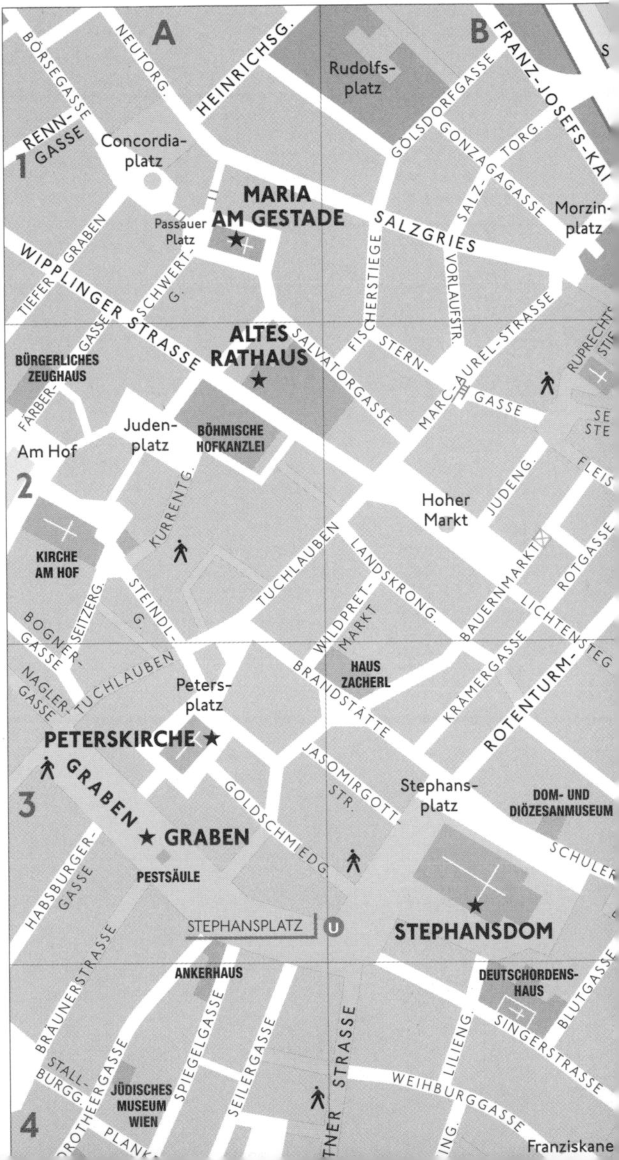

A **B**

Rudolfs-platz

BORSEGASSE

NEUTORG

HEINRICHSG.

FRANZ-JOSEFS-KAI

RENN-GASSE **1** Concordia-platz

GOLSDORFGASSE

GONZAGAGASSE

SALZ-TORG.

Morzin-platz

MARIA AM GESTADE

Passauer Platz ★

SALZGRIES

TIEFER GRABEN

WIPPLINGER STRASSE

SCHWERT-G.

FISCHERSTIEGE

VORLAUFSTR.

MARC-AUREL-STRASSE

ALTES RATHAUS ★

SALVATORGASSE

STERN-GASSE

RUPRECHT-STIE

BÜRGERLICHES ZEUGHAUS

FARBER-GASSE

Juden-platz

BÖHMISCHE HOFKANZLEI

JUDENG.

SE STE

FLEIS

Am Hof

2 **KIRCHE AM HOF**

KURRENTG.

Hoher Markt

BOGNER-GASSE

SEITZERG.

STEINDL-G.

TUCHLAUBEN

LANDSKRONG.

WILDPRET-MARKT

BAUERNMARKT

ROTGASSE

LICHTENSTEG

NAGLER-GASSE

TUCHLAUBEN

Peters-platz

BRANDSTÄTTE

HAUS ZACHERL

KRÄMERGASSE

ROTENTURM

PETERSKIRCHE ★

3 ★ **GRABEN**

HABSBURGER-GASSE

GRABEN

GOLDSCHMIEDG.

JASOMIRGOTT-STR.

Stephans-platz

DOM- UND DIÖZESANMUSEUM

SCHULER

PESTSÄULE

STEPHANSPLATZ Ⓤ

STEPHANSDOM ★

ANKERHAUS

DEUTSCHORDENS-HAUS

BLUTGASSE

BRAUNERSTRASSE

SPIEGELGASSE

SEILERGASSE

KÄRNTNER STRASSE

LILIENG.

SINGERSTRASSE

4

STALLBURGG.

DOROTHEERGASSE

PLANK.

JÜDISCHES MUSEUM WIEN

WEIHBURGGASSE

ING.

Franziskane

Destroyed and rebuilt many times, St Stephen's Cathedral (or 'Stiffl' to the Viennese) looks upon the medieval city, in whose alleys and passageways you will find numerous quiet cafés. The Hoher Markt, a former Roman forum where Marcus Aurelius is said to have died in AD180, is the city's oldest marketplace. It is close to the Bermuda Dreieck (triangle), the bar district and a favorite nocturnal haunt. Going off Stephensplatz is Vienna's other famous landmark and smartest promenade, Graben, a former Roman dike filled in and levelled in the 13th century. Look for baroque fountains and statues on almost every street corner, illuminated by the city lights.

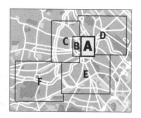

TOKO RI

WRENKH - WIENER KOCHSALON

RESTAURANTS

Würstelstand am Hohen Markt (**A** B2)
→ *Hoher Markt*
Daily 7am–4am
Peckish in the middle of the night? This *Würstelstand* sells the best sausages in Vienna. Choose from *Tiroler*, *Frankfurter* or the famous *Käsekrainer* (dripping with cheese), accompanied by slices of bread and lashings of *Senf* (mild mustard). €1.85–3.15.

Da Capo (**A** C4)
→ *Schulerstrasse 18*
Tel. 512 44 91
Daily 11.30am–11.45pm
Homemade pasta, buffet of antipasti and wide selection of pizzas cooked in a wood-fired oven, served in beautiful vaulted rooms with exposed stonework, frescos and bas-reliefs. Terrace in summer. Entrées €9–24.

Café Korb (**A** A3)
→ *Brandstätte 9*
Tel. 533 72 15; Mon-Sat 8am–midnight; Sun 10am–11pm
Retro and trendy, a grand café decorated in 1960s style with lino on the floor, heavenly comfy, soft velvet seats and waiters in long white aprons. After a bowl of heart-warming

soup, how about a game of skittles in the basement? Entrées €9–16.

Toko Ri (**A** B1)
→ *Salztorgasse 4; Tel. 532 77 77; Daily 11am–11pm*
A massive aquarium stands between diners and the kitchen, where excellent sushi, sashimi and other Japanese delicacies are being made. Entrées €10–17.

Restaurant Wrenkh - Wiener Kochsalon (**A** B2)
→ *Bauernmarkt 10; Tel. 533 15 26; Mon-Fri noon–4pm, 6–10pm; Sat 6–10pm*
A renowned vegetarian restaurant whose reputation rests on the talent of the Wenkh family. Their menu is based on the rather esoteric concept of three tastes to induce energy, balance and beauty. On the plate and in your mouth, however, this innovative, delicious cuisine suddenly makes sense. They also organize cooking classes. Entrées €10–19.50.

Plachutta (**A** D4)
→ *Wollzeile 38; Tel. 512 15 77; Daily 11.30am–11.15pm*
Decorated in elegant green and yellow tones, this is *the* place to enjoy the city's best *Tafelspitz*,

ORGY & BESS   MEINL AM GRABEN   ROSEN & CO

served with sautéed potatoes, chopped apple and horseradish purée in a chive sauce. Plachutta serves no less than ten variations of the classic Viennese dish, which was the favorite of Emperor Franz Josef throughout his reign. Entrées €15–25.

CAFÉS, BARS, CLUBS

Diglas (A C3)
→ *Wollzeile 10; Tel. 512 57 65*
Daily 7am–11pm
With its mouthwatering *Mehlspeisen* (Viennese cakes), its selection of newspapers, its waiters in suits and its clientele of demanding regulars – it has all the ingredients of the traditional beloved Viennese café. Copious Viennese breakfast.

Kleines Café (A B4)
→ *Franziskanerplatz 3*
Daily 10am–2am
With soft lights, tinted mirrors and a Chesterfield sofas, this is a cozy little café, popular with a quieter kind of night owl. Delicious snacks.

Café Alt Wien (A C3)
→ *Bäckerstrasse 9*
Tel. 512 52 22; Daily 10am–2am (4am Fri-Sat)
This noisy bar with red curtains and walls plastered with posters is

where the alternative youth scene likes to meet. Large selection of spirits, from Chivas to Cointreau.

Wunderbar (A D3)
→ *Schönlaterngasse 8*
Tel. 512 79 89
Daily 5pm–2am
Off the beaten track, a bar decorated by hip designer Hermann Czech, with iron arches and concealed toilets. Funk music, a laid-back ambience, and a slightly upmarket clientele.

Bermuda Dreieck
→ *Triangle formed by Hoher Markt (**A** B2), Hauptpost (**A** D2) and Franziskanerplatz (**A** B4)*
The streets of the 'Bermuda Triangle', packed with bars and other nightspots, are a favorite rendezvous for the city's party people.

Jazzland (A C1)
→ *Franz-Josefs-Kai 29*
Tel. 533 25 75; Mon-Sat 7pm–1am (live band 9pm)
Blues, boogie, swing at Vienna's oldest jazz venue.

New York New York (A B5)
→ *Annagasse 8; Tel. 513 86 51; Tue-Fri 5pm–2am (3am Fri); Sat 8pm– 3am*
This tiny bar seems to come from another time and place. Good cocktails and a soundtrack of

classic American jazz, including the inevitable *New York, New York,* which is played every night.

Porgy & Bess (A C4)
→ *Riemergasse 11*
Tel. 512 88 11; Daily 7.30pm–2am (live music 8.30pm)
This former cinema and one of Vienna's best jazz venues has been successfully revamped. It still has excellent acoustics and, now, a large stage for modern jazz bands. After the show, the stalls become a dance floor for late night clubbing.

SHOPPING

Meinl am Graben (A A3)
→ *Graben 19; Tel. 532 33 34 Mon-Fri 8am–7.30pm; Sat 9am–6pm*
Behind an extraordinary façade is Vienna's most prestigious gourmet food store – extensive deli counter with a vast choice of sausages, cheeses, delicious Viennese cakes, endless shelves of Austrian wines and specialties from around the world.

Zauberklingl (A A5)
→ *Führichgasse 4*
Tel. 512 68 68; Mon-Sat 9.30am–6pm (5pm Sat)
An extraordinary shop

selling magic tricks of all kinds. It has been here since 1876 and is run by a magician. There are clown outfits, packs of trick cards, white rabbits and the famous Chinese rings. But if you buy anything, watch your change like a hawk, for they like to play tricks with that too.

Rosen & Co (A B4)
→ *Weihburggasse 8*
Tel. 513 16 73; Mon-Sat 10am–6pm (5pm Sat)
This upmarket store boasts a superb collection of lovingly presented folk costumes: dirndls (traditional dresses) for women and warm loden capes for men.

Haas & Haas (A B3)
→ *Stephansplatz 4*
Tel. 512 97 70; Mon-Sat 9am–6.30pm (6pm Sat)
A treasure trove for tea lovers, with infusions in every conceivable flavor and delicate terracotta teapots, as well as cookies, drinking chocolate, jam and honey.

Satyr Filmwelt (A B2)
→ *Marc-Aurel-Strasse 5*
Tel. 535 53 26-27; Mon-Sat 10am–7pm (5pm Sat)
Two storeys packed with rare DVDs, books, posters and photos celebrate movies from Austria and beyond.

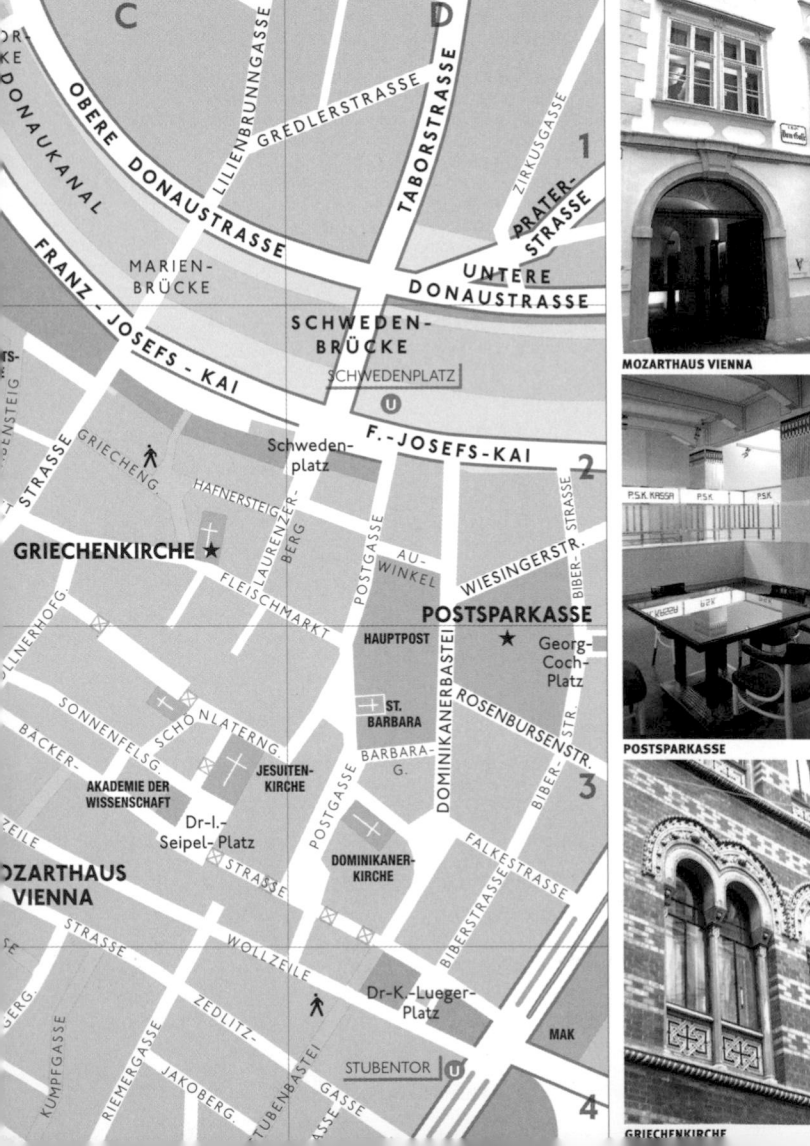

C

D

OBERE DONAUSTRASSE

DONAUKANAL

LILIENBRUNNGASSE

GREDLERSTRASSE

TABORSTRASSE

ZIRKUSGASSE

PRATER-
STRASSE

1

FRANZ - JOSEFS - KAI

MARIEN-
BRÜCKE

UNTERE
DONAUSTRASSE

SCHWEDEN-
BRÜCKE

SCHWEDEN-
BRÜCKE

SCHWEDENPLATZ

Ⓤ

F.-JOSEFS-KAI

Schweden-
platz

2

STRASSE

GRIECHENG.

HAFNERSTEIGERBERG

LAURENZERBERG

FLEISCHMARKT

POSTGASSE

AU-
WINKEL

WIESINGERSTR.

BIBERSTRASSE

GRIECHENKIRCHE ★

POSTSPARKASSE

HAUPTPOST

★ Georg-
Coch-
Platz

ÖLLNERHOFG.

SONNENFELSG.

SCHONLATERNG.

ST.
BARBARA

DOMINIKANERBASTEI

ROSENBURSENSTR.

BIBER- STR.

BACKER-

AKADEMIE DER
WISSENSCHAFT

JESUITEN-
KIRCHE

BARBARA-
G.

POSTGASSE

3

ZEILE

Dr-I.-
Seipel- Platz

STRASSE

DOMINIKANER-
KIRCHE

FALKESTRASSE

BIBERSTRASSE

MOZARTHAUS
VIENNA

STRASSE

WOLLZEILE

BERG

ZEDLITZ-

Dr-K.-Lueger-
Platz

MAK

4

KUMPFGASSE

RIEMERGASSE

STUBENBASTEI

JAKOBERG

GASSE

STUBENTOR Ⓤ

MOZARTHAUS VIENNA

P.S.K. KASSA   P.S.K.   P.S.K.

POSTSPARKASSE

GRIECHENKIRCHE

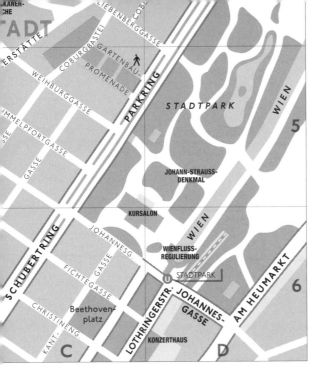

ALTES RATHAUS

MARIA AM GESTADE

Map E ▼

w dedicated to music, it
ouses the museum of the
mous orchestra, where
u can listen to the great
ennese classics by
rauss and others. Try out
e rather fun 'sound arena'
the top floor.

Mozarthaus
Venna (A C3)
→ Domgasse 5
. 512 17 91; Daily 10am–7pm
e house where Mozart
ed from 1784 to 1787,
hen he was at the peak of
s career, and where he
mposed The Marriage of
aro (1786). A few pieces
furniture remain from
ozart's sojourn in the city:
ese are on display in the

reconstruction of his
apartment on the first floor.
Musical exhibition on the
second: scores, busts of
musicians of the era. On the
third floor is a history of
Mozart and his times.

★ Postsparkasse (A D3)
→ Georg-Coch-Platz 2
Tel. 534 53 33 088
Mon-Sat 9am–5pm (10am Sat)
Otto Wagner's savings
bank, built in a record time
of three years, boldly
combines functionalism
and estheticism. The simple
façade, crowned with
winged statues of victory, is
clad with marble, set off by
industrial materials and
nails left open to view.

Inside are an impressive
banking hall and a small
museum devoted to Wagner.

★ Griechenkirche (A C2)
→ Fleischmarkt 13; Tel. 533 29
65; Mon-Fri 9am–2pm
A striking red-brick Greek
Orthodox church, dating to
the 18th and 19th centuries.
Cherub-topped columns
adorn the entrance which
leads to the sanctuary with
its splendid oriental carpets
and icon-covered walls.
Note the magnificent crystal
chandelier.

★ Altes Rathaus (A A2)
→ Wipplinger Strasse 6-8
The former city hall (1699).
Behind the two portals
presided over by Justice and

Kindness, is the former
municipal council chamber,
a solemn hall with caryatids
and a fine stucco decor
featuring plant motifs.
Sunny central courtyard
with an Andromeda fountain
(1741, George R. Donner).

★ Maria
am Gestade (A A1)
→ Salvatorgasse 12; Tel. 533
95 94; Daily 8am–6pm
This slender, beautiful
church, only 12 feet wide,
is a masterpiece of 14th-
century Flamboyant Gothic,
with a magnificent open-
work spire (1688), beautiful
sculpted stone over the
doorway, and delicate
ribbed vaults.

SCHATZKAMMER

SPANISCHE HOFREITSCHULE

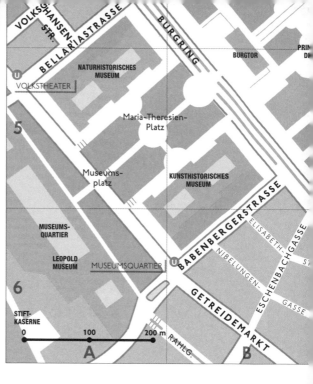

★ **Am Hof** (B C2)
→ *Market: Fri-Sat 10am–8pm (March-Nov)*
All that remains of the original Babenberg Castle, residence of the Duke of Ostmark (1135–1246), is the name: 'Am Hof' or 'at the royal court'. At the center of this pretty cobblestoned square stands the Virgin's Pillar (1667). To the east is the church of the Nine Choirs of Angels, with its baroque balustrade with flame ornaments, and an elegant fire station (16th century) housed in the former old town arsenal. The square is a somewhat solemn place and yet it retains a village air about it, especially on market day.

★ **Freyung** (B C2)
→ *Farmers' market: Tue-Thu 10am–6.30pm (May-Oct)*
This non-symmetrical square lies at the heart of the district once inhabited by Vienna's feudal lords. Here stand the imposing Scottish convent and church with its fine baroque interior, where strangers and thieves were granted asylum and freedom (*frei* means free). See also the Daun-Kinsky Palace (1716), reputedly one of Hildebrandt's most beautiful buildings; and the Ferstel Palace (1860), whose delicately colored passage leads into Herrengasse (the lords' street).

★ **Hofburg** (B C4)
→ *Michaelerplatz Tel. 533 75 70; Apartments and museum: daily 9am–5.30pm*
The seat of power of the Habsburgs, built in the 13th century then continually enlarged until the fall of the monarchy in 1918. Enter via the monumental St Michael's Portal, with its copper dome and statues of Hercules triumphant. Move on to the Imperial Apartments, whose purple hangings and gilt stucco stand out in stark contrast to the white walls. The famous portrait of Elizabe of Austria, or Sissi, as queen of Hungary, by Geo Raab, invites you to visit Sissi Museum: dresses, personal items and letter tell the story of her short but remarkable life.

★ **Schatzkammer** (B C
→ *Schweitzerhof; Tel. 525 2 40; Wed-Mon 10am–6pm*
The Imperial Treasury contains the dazzling symbols of spiritual and temporal power: the crow of the Holy Roman Empire (10th century) studded with precious stones and embellished with a cross, golden globe and liturgical objects.

HOFBURG

FREYUNG

AM HOF

Map labels:

SCH

ERZHERZOG-KARL-
DENKMAL

STRASSE

Schmerling-
platz

PARLAMENT

Ballhaus-
platz

BRUC

BUNDES-
KANZLERAMT

METASTASIOG.

LÖWELSTRASSE

VOLKSGARTEN

D R - K A R L - R E N N E R - R I N G

MINORITENK

STADTPALAIS
LIECHTENSTEIN

Josef-
Meinrad-
platz

REICHSRATS-

PARK

PALAIS
STARHEMBERG

★ BURGTHEATER

BANKGAS

SCHENKEN
STR.

Rathaus-
platz

LÖWELSTR.

RATHAUS

ROSENG

SCHENKEN

D R - K A R L - L U E G E R - R I N G

TEINFALTSTRASSE

FELDERSTR.

OPPOLZERG

SCHREYVOGELG

KIN
PAL

R A T H A U S -

PASQUALATI-
HAUS

STRASSE

MÖLKER-
BASTEI

MÖLKER
STEIG

EBENDORFER-

LIEBIGG

STRASSE

HEL
GASSE

SCHOTTEN-

UNIVERSITÄT

BASTEI

RING

UNIVERSITÄTSSTRASSE

SCHOTTEN-
RING

SCHOTTENGASSE

SIGMUND-FREUD-
PARK

B

A

1

2

3

4

The Freyung was once the antechamber to imperial power as it provided the setting for the haughty palaces of the nobility. Running off this square is an attractive labyrinth of alleyways converging on the imposing Hofburg Palace. The monarchy is now a thing of the past, but the country's destiny is still determined near the palace, in the secluded Minoritenplatz, the headquarters of the federal chancellery. The Hofburg, a succession of wings (*Trakt*) and courtyards studded with greenery, forms a veritable 'inner city', rounded off by the Burgtheater and Staatsoper, two cultural hotspots beloved by Viennese.

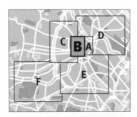

ESTERHÁZYKELLER

DO & CO

RESTAURANTS

Trzesniewski (**B** D4)
→ *Dorotheergasse 1*
Tel. 512 32 91; Mon-Fri 9am–7.30pm; Sat 9am–5pm
An irresistible selection of appetizers, *Aufstrichbrote*, are small bread slices spread with sardines and onions, crab and egg, salami, etc. From €1.

Esterházykeller (**B** C3)
→ *Haarhof 1; Tel. 533 34 82*
Daily 11am–11pm
A steep staircase leads down to a maze of former wine cellars where you can feast on traditional family cooking (breaded chicken, beef patties, black pudding etc.) and wines from the Eisenstadt estate (Burgenland). Entrées €6–10.

DO & CO (**B** D5)
→ *Albertinaplatz 1; Tel. 532 96 69; Daily 9am–midnight*
Huge mirrors, red marble, caramel-colored leather seats are some of the eye-catching features of the museum's elegant restaurant. On the menu, Viennese cuisine with a Mediterranean twist. Wonderful terrace looking at the Staatsoper in summer. Entrées €15–28.

Zum Schwarzen Kameel (**B** D2)
→ *Bognergasse 5*
Tel. 533 81 25; Mon-Sat noon–2.30pm, 6–10.30pm
Waiters in swallow-tail coats and colorful plates on the wall are part of the charm of this timeless Viennese institution, which recalls the days of high society and the Empire. *Gourmets* (sophisticated snacks) to eat at the counter in the bar area or a more elaborate menu in the Art Deco restaurant. Entrées €20–45.

Rote Bar (**B** D5)
→ *Hotel Sacher, Philharmonikerstrasse 4*
Tel. 514 56 840
Daily noon–10.30pm
Seating on plush red banquettes and chairs, gazing at the dark red walls where Sacher family portraits hang, or at the Staatsoper across the road, you feel as if you'd been sent back to the 19th century. Attentive, discreet service and refined traditional cuisine. Formal dress required (suit jacket supplied if necessary). Entrées €25–40.

RieGi (**B** C3)
→ *Schauflergasse 6*
Tel. 532 91 26; Tue-Sat noon–3pm, 6pm–midnight
A family feel and immaculate design (blue

CAFÉ HAWELKA

NAGY HÜTE

DEMEL

ceiling and abstract paintings in bright colors), serving an interesting take on Mediterranean cuisine. Fine list of international wines. Entrées € 27–48.

CAFÉS

Café Sacher (B D5)
→ *Hotel Sacher, Philharmonikerstrasse 4 Daily 8am–midnight*
This popular café is the place to eat authentic Sachertorte, created by Franz Sacher in 1832. The treat is accompanied by velvety Chantilly cream.

Café Griensteidl (B C3)
→ *Michaelerplatz 2; Tel. 535 26 920; Daily 8am–11.30pm*
Once through the elegant double doors, you have two options: to sit in the first room with a view of the imposing Hofburg, or in the other room, which has two original works by Klimt on the walls and looks out onto the streamlined modern Loos Haus (1912). Don't miss the traditional *Apfelstrudel* (apple pastry with raisins).

Café Central (B C3)
→ *Herrengasse 14 Tel. 533 37 64 26; Daily 7.30am (10am Sun)–10pm; live music 5–10pm*
Another grand café, originally meant to house the stock exchange, hence the vast, circular, glittering room with chandeliers, vaulted ceilings, and tall Gothic columns. The Melange is better here than anywhere else, or there are no less than 16 other varieties of coffee.

Café Landtmann (B B2)
→ *Dr-Karl-Lueger-Ring 4 Tel. 241 00 100 Daily 7.30am–midnight*
With its spacious terrace on the Ring, it was Freud's favorite *kaffeehaus*, and is still the meeting place for the Austrian intelligentsia. The vast rooms are always buzzing for this is where politicians hold court after a session in the nearby Parliament. Good range of hot drinks and specialty coffees. Small theater, The Tribune, in the basement.

Café Hawelka (B D4)
→ *Dorotheergasse 6 Tel. 512 82 30; Wed-Mon 8am–2am (Sun 10am)*
Off the populated Graben and protected from the prying eyes of passers-by, it's rather dark inside, with red old sofas, creaking floorboards, yellowing walls and a sleepy stove. Apart from the piles of daily newspapers nothing seems to have changed since the café opened in 1945.

CLUB

Volksgarten (B B4)
→ *Burgring; Tue 9pm–2am; Thu-Sat 11pm–dawn*
A vast complex at one entrance of the imperial gardens, with a nightclub whose roof opens to dance under the stars and a summer garden. Eclectic program: reggae, RnB, house.

SHOPPING

Lederleitner (B B1)
→ *Römische Markthalle, Schottenring 16 Tel. 532 06 77; Mon-Fri 10am–8pm; Sat 9am–5pm*
Browse at leisure among the beautiful plants, waterfalls and exotic blooms of this extraordinary flower shop.

Nagy Hüte (B B2)
→ *Schottengasse 3 Tel. 405 66 29 22; Mon-Sat 10am–6pm (Sat 5pm)*
Hats in all shapes and sizes, from sports caps to sophisticated fur models.

Schiepek (B B2)
→ *Teinfaltstrasse 3 Tel. 533 15 75; Mon-Sat 10.30am–6.30pm (5pm Sat)*
Create your own jewelry from a choice of thousand and one colors, shapes and materials, which is then skillfully assembled

by four deft assistants.

Demel (B C3)
→ *Kohlmarkt 14; Tel. 535 17 170; Daily 9am–7pm*
Former imperial bakers and, with the Sacher, the only possessor of the torte secret recipe, the Demel is worth a visit. Chocolates, cakes, jams, preserves – all are delicious. Take out or sit down in the café side of this beautiful, heavily gilded shop.

Xocolat (B C2)
→ *Freyung 2; Mon-Fri 9.30am–6.30pm; Sat 10am–6pm; Sun noon–5pm*
Attractively presented chocolate in original permutations: with herbs, filled with Apfelstrudel or Sacher-Torte, and more.

Dorotheum (B D4)
→ *Dorotheergasse 17 Tel. 515 600; Mon-Fri 10am–6pm; Sat 9am–5pm*
One of the biggest auction houses in the world inside a vast neo-baroque palace (1901).

Meinl am Graben (B D3)
→ *Graben 19; Tel. 532 3334 Mon-Sat 8.30am–10pm*
Vienna's extraordinary gourmet food hall. If 400 types of cheese don't impress look to the caviar, truffles and rare wines. High-end restaurant upstairs, or try one of the deli's meals-to-go.

▲ Map A

NEUE BURG

ALBERTINA

NATIONALBIBLIOTHEK

▼ Map D

KAMMER ★

Josefs-

★ Schweizerhof

SPANISCHE HOFREITSCHULE

REITSCHUL

STALLBURG

HOFBURG ★

St. MICHAEL

Michaeler-platz

LOOSHAUS

KOHLMARKT

CHAUFLERG.

INNERE STADT

ANKERHAUS

PESTSÄULE

GRABEN

SEILERGASSE

SPIEGELGASSE

JÜDISCHES MUSEUM WIEN

HEERGASSE

BRAUNERSTRASSE

HABSBURGERGASSE

STALLBURG

PETERS-KIRCHE

Peters-platz

PALAIS ESTERHAZY

HAARHOF

WALLNER-STRASSE

ESTERHAZY

HERRENGASSE

HERREN-

LEOPOLD-BRG-GASSE

ERDSTERR. HANDHAUS

ANHEN-

AUSG.

STRAUCHGASSE

FERRENGASSE

BOGNERGASSE

NAGLERGASSE

TUCHLAUBEN

SEITZERG.

STEINDLG.

UHRENMUSEUM

KIRCHE AM HOF

KURRENTG.

PALAIS FERSTEL

FREYUNG

PALAIS HARRACH

AM HOF ★

TIEFER

PALAIS SCHÖNBORN-BATTHYANY

BÜRGERLICHES ZEUGHAUS

BÖHMISCHE HOFKANZLEI

Juden-platz

GRABEN

RENNGASSE

SCHOTTEN-KIRCHE

ALTES RATHAUS

STRASSE

WIPPLINGER

FÄRBER-GASSE

FÄRBER-G.

SCHOTTENSTIFT

MARIA AM GESTADE

Passauer platz

Concordia-platz

SALZ-GRIES

HEINRICHSG.

WIPPLINGER STR.

RENNGASSE

BÖRSEGASSE

HOHENSTAUFEN GASSE

FESTRASSE

ROCKH-

UNIVERSITÄT JURIDICUM

Börse-platz

WIPPLINGER STR.

D

C

▼ Map D

STAATSOPER

BURGTHEATER

Map E ▼

Spanische ~freitschule (**B** C4)
*Reitschulgasse 2
~. 533 90 32; Lipizzaner
~seum: Tue-Sun 9am–6pm*
~e prestigious Spanish
~ding School, founded in
~72, is one of the last to
~actice the ancient
~uestrian art. Watch one
~ the performances to
~usic by the famous white
~izzan horses in the
~nter manège designed
~ Fischer von Erlach.

Nationalbibliothek
~ C4)
*Josefsplatz 1; Tel. 534 10
~e-Sun 10am–6pm (9pm Thu)*
~e of the finest baroque
~raries in the world (1726),

commissioned by Charles VI,
whose statue stands in the
center of the magnificent
'splendor hall' (*Prunksaal*).
The cupola was decorated
by Daniel Gran with frescos
glorifying the emperor,
several splendid globes by
Coronelli (1693), and a vast
collection of over 200,000
leather-bound books.

★ Albertina (**B** D5)
→ *Albertinaplatz 1; Tel. 534 83
Daily 10am–6pm (9pm Wed)*
It houses an impressive
graphic arts collection that
includes works by some of
the greatest artists: Dürer
(including the 500-year-old
Hare), Raphael, Rubens,
Goya, Klimt and Picasso.

★ Neue Burg (**B** C5)
→ *Heldenplatz; Tel. 525 24 403
Mon, Wed-Sun 10am–6pm*
The most recent wing to
be added to the Hofburg
(1914), the New Palace is
an imposing edifice built
on a curve. It contains the
Ephesus Museum which
houses the great frieze
from the Parthian
monument, collections of
early musical instruments,
of weapons and armor, a
Papyrus Museum and
Ethnography Museum.

★ Staatsoper (**B** D6)
→ *Opernring 2; Tel. 514 4422
50 (call about guided tours)*
One of the three biggest
opera houses in the world,

it was rebuilt after World
War 2 and reopened in
1955, when Austria
regained its sovereignty.
The grand staircase (1869)
is the only part, along with
the foyer, to have survived
the bombing.

★ Burgtheater (**B** B2)
→ *Dr.-K.-Lueger-Ring 2
Tel. 514 44 4140
Visit daily 3pm*
The former court theater
(1741) was replaced in
1888 by this elegant
building with two extensive
wings. Each has a
monumental staircase – the
court did not mingle with
the public – decorated with
frescos by Klimt.

LEOPOLD MUSEUM

PARLAMENT

★ Kunsthistorisches Museum (C D5)

→ *Maria-Theresien-Platz*
Tel. 525 240; Tue–Sun
10am–6pm (9pm Thu)
Testimony to the Habsburgs'
role as patrons of the arts,
this huge, elaborate edifice
(1891) is one of Europe's
major art museums. It
comprises Greek and
Roman antiquities;
Egyptian antiquities with a
splendid sarcophagus hall;
sculpture and decorative
arts; and an extraordinary
painting collection with no
less than 15 works by
Bruegel – a quarter of his
œuvre – including *Hunters
in the Snow* (1565).

★ Naturhistorisches Museum (C D5)

→ *Burgring 7; Tel. 521 77*
Wed–Mon 9am–6.30pm
(9pm Wed)
This Natural History Museum
(1889), an almost perfect
replica of the neighboring
Kunsthistorisches, houses
the collections of François-
Étienne de Lorraine,
preserved exactly as he
arranged them. On the
ground floor: minerals and
meteorites; on the first and
second floors: fossils,
stuffed animals,
reconstructions of dinosaurs
and prehistoric objects,
including the famous 4,000-
year-old Venus of Willendorf.

★ Museumsquartier (C D5-6)

→ *Museumsplatz 1*
Tel. 0820 600 600
The Museumquartier Wien
(MQW) is one of the largest
cultural areas in the world,
and is dedicated to modern
art. Behind the long façade
of the former imperial
stables, designed by Fischer
von Erlach (1723), is a set of
streamlined buildings,
erected in 2001: the
imposing Museum of
Modern Art (MUMOK), built
entirely of basalt; the
Leopold Museum, made of
limestone; and the
revamped Winter
Manège. Plus a museum of

childhood, an architecture
center and a dancing scho

★ Leopold Museum (C D5

→ *Wed–Mon 10am–6pm*
(9pm Thu)
This collection, built up
by the art lover Rudolf
Leopold, contains 5,500
works by Austrian masters
Light-filled galleries set of
the great classics by Klimt
Kokoschka and Schiele.

★ Parlament (C D4)

→ *Dr.-Karl-Lueger-Ring 3*
Tel. 401 102 400 (tours)
The parliament building,
(1883) with its Corinthian
columns, pronaos and
Pallas Athene fountain,
takes its inspiration from
classical Greek temples, i

C

MUSEUMSQUARTIER

NATURHISTORISCHES MUSEUM

KUNSTHISTORISCHES MUSEUM

PIARIST KIRCH

MARIA TREU

KLOST

LERCHENGASSE

PFEIL-GASSE

LENAUGASSE

NTHALERGASSE

BLINDEN-INSTITUT

GÜRTEL

4

JOSEFSTÄDTER

GÜRTEL

FUHRMANNSG.

SCHÖNBORNG.

SKODAGASSE

Hamerling-platz

JOSEFSTÄDTER STR.

JOSEFSTÄDTER STR.

FLORIANI-GASSE

SCHLÖSINGER-platz

Benno-platz

Uhlplatz

U

SCHÖNBORNG.

SKODAGASSE

ALBERTG.

LAUDON- GASSE

HERNALSER

SCHELLHAMMER GASSE

GASSE

VERONIKA-GASSE

KOCH-GASSE

LEDERER-

LAUD

DOROTHEUM

FELDGASSE

BEN-NOG.

BREITENFELDER G.

Albert-platz

HERNALSER GTL.

PAYER-FIAKER-MUSEUM

BRUNNEN-GASSE

3

OTTAKRINGER STR.

GASSE

ALSER

ALSER STR.

PELIKANG.

ALSER GASSE

GEBLER-GASSE

GASSE

HÖFERG.

MARIANNEN-GASSE

KINDERSPITALG.

KINDERSPITAL

Zimmermann-platz

U

HERNALSER HAUPTSTR.

ALLGEMEINE POLIKLINIK

LAZARETTGASSE

ALSER STRASSE

JÖRGERSTRASSE

2

BÖRSCHKEGASSE

KRANKENANSTALT GOLDENES KREUZ

WÄHRINGER

WÄHRINGER GTL.

STRINGGASSE

SCHRINGGASSE

BEHEIMGASSE

DEM-GASSE

BLUMEN-GASSE

ALLGEMEINES KRANKENHAUS

WÄHRINGER GTL.

GASSE

THERESIENGASSE

MARTINSTRASSE

SCHUMANN-G.

HILDEBRAND

ANTONIGASSE

MICHELBEUERN AKH

U

WÄHRINGER

WÄHRINGER GÜRTEL

KUTSCHKERGASSE

H.-SACHS-GASSE

STAUD

CANONGASSE

SEMPER-STR.

THERESIENGASSE

SCHOPENHAUERSTRASSE

KREUZGASSE

LEITERMAYERGASSE

TESCHNER-G.

MARTINSTRASSE

1

STAUDGASSE

SCHULGASSE

SCHOPENHAUER-G.

SCHUL-GASSE

SCHUBERT-PARK

VOLK

WÄHRINGER GÜRTEL

U

WÄHRINGER STR

VOLKSOPER

WÄHRINGER STRASSE

WÄHRINGER

B

A

In 1857, much later than other capital cities, Vienna pulled down its ancient ramparts. Magnificent buildings in the Historicist style sprang up around the 'Ring'. Alive with people, cars and trams, this thoroughfare is the lifeblood of the city. To the west, the scene changes – the elegant buildings give way to a less disciplined, more eclectic style. There are the bars and fashionable shops of Neubau; a hive of cultural activity in Spittleberg; the bourgeois calm of Josefstadt; and the lively student district of Alsergrund. Further away, among the arcades of the Gürtel, or 'working-class Ring', are the trendy night spots favored today by the young Viennese.

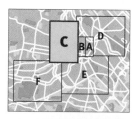

KENT

DER WIENER DEEWAN

RESTAURANTS

Ronahi (C A6)
→ *Schottenfeldgasse 18*
Tel. 944 03 33; Daily 10am (5pm Sun)–11pm
A haven of tranquillity amid the hubbub of the Neubau. The upstairs area with its comfortable couches and Oriental carpets provides the perfect setting for enjoying the Syrian and Kurdish specialties on offer. Entrées €4–9.

Kent (C A3)
→ *Brunnengasse 67*
Tel. 405 91 73
Daily 6am–2am
A popular meeting-place, especially for the local Turkish community, it's always busy, and the budget-price food is always good. Entrées €7–10.

Amerlingbeisl (C C5)
→ *Stiftgasse 8*
Tel. 526 16 60
Daily 9am–2am
In the Amerling Haus cultural center in the heart of the Spittleberg neighborhood, this small bistro should satisfy your every whim, be it breakfast (until 3pm) or cocktails (from 5pm). Delicious, healthy food (soups, salads, vegetable gratin with yoghurt, etc.) is

served in the small dining room, or on the very pleasant and leafy paved courtyard. Brunch at the weekend. Entrées €7–11.

Der Wiener Deewan (C D3)
→ *Liechtensteinstrasse 10*
Tel. 925 11 85
Mon-Sat 11am–11pm
This cheap, informal Pakistani buffet has an unusual philosophy: diners can serve themselves as much fish or meat curry as they want and then pay what they think it is worth. Eat in the basement, seated on school chairs, under the light of two globe lamps. Vegan options available. Fixed prices for drinks.

Stomach (C D1)
→ *Seegasse 26*
Tel. 310 20 99; Wed-Sat 6–11.30pm; Sun noon–9pm
Innovative, imaginative Austrian cuisine in a former farmhouse whose decor has remained almost unchanged: uneven floor, ceramic tiled stove. In summer, eat outdoors in the lovely, leafy courtyard. The rare Austrian rosé wines are worth sampling. Entrées €12–20.

Zum Wickerl (C D1)
→ *Porzellangasse 24a*
Tel. 317 7489; Mon-Sat 9am–

DONAU

ECLECTICK

VINOE

midnight (10pm Sat);
Sun 11am–11pm

This traditional café-bistro
with its crackling radio in
one corner and a warm
and friendly atmosphere
is a neighborhood
favorite. The fillet of trout
with mango may not be
traditional local cuisine
but it tastes superb.
Entrées €15.

CAFÉS, BARS

Das Möbel (C C5)
→ Burggasse 10
Tel. 524 94 97
Daily 10am– 1am
A café-gallery where
young designers
showcase their creations,
hence the chairs of all
shapes and sizes, funky
tables and designer
furniture. Everything is for
sale but you could just
have a coffee.

Wirr (C B5)
→ Burggasse 70
Tel. 929 40 50
Mon-Fri 11am–2am(4am
Thu-Fri); Sat-Sun 10am-2am
All the ingredients for a
relaxed night out in a
cheerful environment:
second-hand furniture,
abstract paintings on the
walls, table soccer,
neckties hanging from the
ceiling, a concert space,
light snacks.

Café Europa (C C6)
→ Zollergasse 8
Tel. 526 33 83; Daily
9am–5pm
This café with brightly
colored decor in retro
1950s style is invariably
busy. It serves as a stage
for lively, smoke-shrouded
conversations that are
only interrupted by
sessions from up-and-
coming Austrian DJs.

Donau (C D6)
→ Karl-Schweighofer
Gasse 10; Tel. 523 81 05
Daily 8pm–4am (6am Fri-
Sat, 2am Sun)
The anonymous door to
the Donau leads to the
heart of the Viennese
underground. Its high
vaulted ceilings add a
cathedral-like grandeur to
the frenetic music of the
DJs, set off by projections
of Communist imagery.

7 Stern (C C6)
→ Siebensterngasse 31
Tel. 699 152 36 157
Mon-Sat 4pm–2am
Bright lights and heated
discussions emanate
from the back room of
this bar, which is always
packed. All that remains
of its checkered past (it
was a Gestapo HQ then
home to the Communist
news-paper Volksstimme)
is the Soviet star above
the bar.

Café Stein (C C1)
→ Währinger Strasse 6–8
Tel. 319 72 41
Daily 7am (9am Sun)–1am
A hip, multifaceted bar
that plays host to
photograph exhibitions
and classical music
concerts, and serves
breakfast until 8pm.

CULTURAL CENTER

WUK (C C1)
→ Währinger Strasse 59
Tel. 401 210; wuk.at
Founded in 1981 this huge
40,000-square feet
cultural center is still
thriving. Art galleries, a
movie theater, a theater,
and a large auditorium
hosting an excellent
program of music events.

SHOPPING

Lomo-Shop (C D5)
→ Museumsquartier
Tel. 523 70 16; Daily 1–7pm
In the heart of the
Kunsthalle, top young
local talent designs for
the Lomographie label.

Neubau
A magnet for fashion
victims!

Boutik 54 (C B5)
→ Neubaugasse 54
Tel. 525 55 1; Mon-Sat
10am–7pm (6pm Sat)
Vintage and bohemian

clothes for the hipsters
of Neubau.

Be a good girl (C B6)
→ Westbahnstrasse 5a
Tue-Sat 10am–7pm
(4pm Sat)
Ready-to-wear clothing,
accessories and a
hairdresser's.

Eclectick (C C6)
→ Lindengasse 22
Tel. 890 4883; Mon-Sat
noon–7pm (Sat 5pm)
Clothes created by a
Hungarian designer:
outlandish handbags and
patchwork skirts.

Vinoe (C C4)
→ Piaristengasse 35
Tel. 402 09 61; Mon-Fri 4–
7.30pm; Sat 10am–12.30pm
Informal wine-tasting
sessions with Mr Rausch,
knowledgeable wine buff.

**Ramsch
und Rosen (C** B6)
→ Neubaugasse 15
Tel. 586 05 20; Mon-Thu
noon–6pm; Fri 10am–4pm
A tiny boutique with soft
pink lighting, selling all
kinds of mementos and
oddities of the 1950s.

Humana (C B5)
→ Lerchenfelder Strasse 45
Tel. 40 25 136; Mon-Sat
11am–6.30pm (5pm Sat)
A fascinating collection
of second-hand clothes
and accessories in garish
colors from the 1960s
and 1970s.

▲ Maps B/D

SIGMUND-FREUD-MUSEUM

VOTIVKIRCHE

RATHAUS

24

LIECHTENSTEIN MUSEUM

PIARISTENKIRCHE

Map E ▼

oute to Athenian mocracy. The grandiose erior holds statues of eek gods, a peristyle tirely covered in marble d monolithic columns.

Rathaus (C C4)
→ *Rathausplatz; Tel. 525 50 rs Mon, Wed, Fri: 1pm*
e massive neo-Gothic y hall (1883) is a dmark, with its 325-foot ver and statue of the *thausmann*, a knight aring a standard. In front the building are seven urtyards where large-ale public events are d: a giant Christmas rket, and open-air operas d movies in summer.

★ **Votivkirche (C** D3)
→ *Rooseveltplatz*
Tel. 406 11 92; Tue-Sat 9am–1pm, 4–6pm; Sun 9am–1pm
A wonderful pastiche of a Gothic cathedral (1855–79) designed by Heinrich von Ferstel. This majestic Viennese church, built to commemorate the failed attempt to assassinate Franz-Joseph (1853), boasts magnificent stained-glass windows.

★ **Sigmund-Freud-Museum (C** D2)
→ *Berggasse 19*
Tel. 319 1596; Daily 9am–5pm (6pm in summer)
The father of psychoanalysis (1856–1939) lived in this

apartment from 1891 until his exile to London (1938). Documents in his waiting and consultation rooms, a collection of antique statuettes, and family movies with a commentary by Freud's daughter Anna. A fascinating glimpse into the life of the great man.

★ **Liechtenstein Museum (C** D1)
→ *Fürstengasse 1; Tel. 319 57 67; Fri-Tue 9am–8pm*
The rich collection of the princes of Liechtenstein, moved out of the Garden Palace (17th–18th century) in 1945, was reinstated in 2004. Works are hung in big, airy rooms and include

Renaissance to Austrian Romanticist masterpieces by, among others, Raphael, Rembrandt, Rubens and Waldmüller.

★ **Piaristenkirche (C** B4)
→ *Jodok-Fink-Platz*
Mon-Sat 7–9am, 6–8pm (7.30pm Tue, Thu, Sat); Sun 7am–noon, 6–8pm
Standing in a tree-lined square with a façade that is part Renaissance and part baroque is the 18th-century Piarist Church of Mary the Faithful, an order which educated poor children. A stunning, light-flooded nave illuminates the frescos (1752–53) by Maulbertsch.

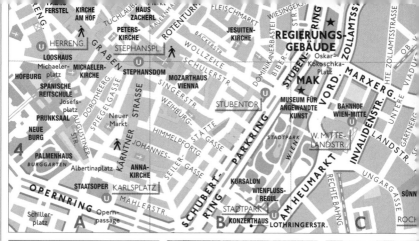

RIESENRAD

STRAUSS-HAUS

WIENER KRIMINALMUSEUM

★ **MAK (D** C4)
→ *Stubenring 5*
Tel. 712 80 00; Tue-Sun
10am–6pm (midnight Tue)
One of Europe's oldest
museums of decorative arts
(1864), it has an unusual
layout: the precious objects
are classified according to
style and material. Exhibits
include the ubiquitous
Thonet curved beech chair
(1841), a series of drawings
by Klimt in the vast
Jugendstil gallery, and
works by the Wiener
Werkstätte – the immensely
influential Viennese
workshops founded by
Kolomann Moser and Josef
Hoffmann (1903), who

advocated democratizing
the decorative arts.
★ **Regierungsgebäude**
(D C3)
→ *Stubenring 1*
The former Ministry of
War (1913) stands like a
battleship parading its
military decorations: a huge
bronze eagle eyeing the
Ring from the top of the
cornice, angels ready for
battle, busts of worthy
generals and, in front, an
equestrian statue (1892)
of Marshal Radetzky.
★ **KunstHausWien (D** D3)
→ *Untere Weissgerberstr. 13*
Tel. 712 04 95
Daily 10am–7pm
This museum, with a

dreamlike black-and-white
checkerboard façade,
houses the works of the
painter and architect
Friedensreich (Fritz)
Hundertwasser (1928–
2000), who also designed
the building. References to
nature abound and this,
with the rejection of straight
lines and industrial
stereotypes, mark out the
work of the artist.
★ **Hundertwasserhaus**
(D D4)
→ *Kegelgasse 36–38*
This public housing project
(1985) designed by the
inventive Hundertwasser
is a kaleidoscope of colors
and materials, a homage

to eclecticism and
imagination: trees sprout
from the raised ground and
there are leaning columns
and amazing Byzantine
onion domes. Behind the
mosaic and mirrored faça
the 51 apartments are all
distinct from each other.
★ **Prater (D** F4)
Flanked by tracks for
joggers, walkers and rider
the broad central avenue
(Hauptallee) of the city's
biggest park (3,200 acres
seems endless. It was the
site of the Congress of
Vienna in 1815 and has
now become a byword
for leisure: fairground
attractions, Rapid Vienna

D

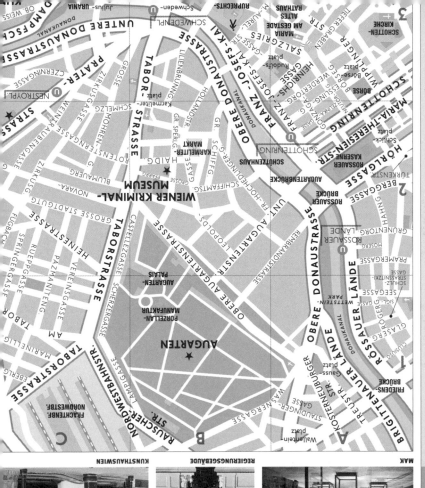

OB WEISS

DAMPFSCH

Julius-URANIA

Schweden-

SCHWEDENPL.

M.-AUREL-

RUPRECHTS-

TIEFER GRABEN

STR

MARIA
AM GESTADE

ALTES
RATHAUS

SCHOTTEN-
KIRCHE

3

DONAUKANAL

UNTERE DONAUSTRASSE

FRANZ-JOSEFS-KAI

SALZGRIES

HEINRICHS-
GASSE

Rudolfs-
platz

TIEFER GRABEN

WIPPLINGER STR

CZERNINGASSE

PRATER-
STRASSE

GROSSE
ZIRKUSGASSE

WEINTR

TABOR-
STRASSE

Karmeliter-
platz

LILIENBRUNNG.

HOLLANDTR.

OBERE DONAUSTRASSE

DONAUKANAL

BÖRSE-
GASSE

WERDERTOR-G

ESSLING

GONZAGA

BÖRSE
platz

WERDERTORG

SCHOTTEN

BÖRSE

WIPPLINGER STR

NESTROYPL.

GR SPERLG

GR.

SCHOTTENRING

SCHOTTENRING

MARIA-THERESIEN-STR

MARIA-THERESIEN-RING

STRASSE

MOHREN-G

SCHMELZ

KARMELITER-
MARKT

ROTENSTERNGASSE

SCHIFFG

SCHIFFG

SCHUTZENHAUS

HÖRLGASSE

ROSSAUER
KASERNE-STR

Schlick-
platz

ZIRKUSG

BLUMAUERG

HAIDG.

GR. PFARRG

KARMELITER-
MARKT

AUGARTENBRÜCKE

TÜRKENSTR

HÖRLGASSE

2

WIENER KRIMINAL-
MUSEUM

FR.-HOCHEDLINGERG.

GR.SCHIFFAMTSG.

UNT. AUGARTENSTR

ROSSAUER
BRÜCKE

BERGGASSE

HAHNG

NOVARA-

GROSSE STADTGUTG

CASTELLEZGASSE

REMBRANDTSTRASSE

REICHSRATSSTRASSE

ROSSAUER LÄNDE

GRÜNENTORG- LÄNDE

MOSER

FLUGBACH

TABORSTRASSE

HEINESTRASSE

VEREINSGASSE

SCHERZERGASSE

OBERE AUGARTENSTR

LEOPOLDS-

PRAMERGASSE

SPRINGERGASSE

RUEPPGASSE

PAZMANITENG

AUGARTEN-
PALAIS

OBERE DONAUSTRASSE

SCHULZ-
STRASSNITZKI-
GASSE

SEEGASSE

AM TABOR

VEREINSGASSE

PORZELLAN-
MANUFAKTUR

WETTSTEIN-
PARK

sigl.-GASSE

GLASERG

ROGERG

MARINELLIG

TABORSTRASSE

RAUSCHERSTR.

AUGARTEN
★

DONAUKANAL

GLASERG

KLUSG

FRÄCHTENBG.
NÖRDWESTER

NÖRDWESTBAHNSTR.

LAMPLGASSE

STAUDINGER-
GASSE

WASNERGASSE

Gauss
platz

FRIEDENS-
BRÜCKE

TREUSTR.

RÖSSAUER LÄNDE

EBERLG

Wallenstein-
platz

KLOSTERNEUBURGER STR.

A

BRIGITTENAU

REGIERUNGSGEBÄUDE

KUNSTHAUSWIEN

MAK

The Ring, which comes to an end in Donaukanal, is bounded to the south by the rushing waters of the Wien, its banks graced by elegant Jugendstil regulation plants designed to hold the river in check. On the other side, Leopoldstadt, which was home to many of the city's Jews until 1938, has preserved its Jewish heritage, while also boasting several long avenues, contemporary-style apartment blocks and the huge Prater Park. Strauss waltzes can be heard inviting visitors to a boat trip down the Danube: as wind blows in from the plain, you will get stunning views of Mount Kalhenberg in the distance, and of the straight watercourse beyond.

BUNKEREI

AERA

RESTAURANTS

Bunkerei (D B1)
→ *Obere Augartenstrasse 1a Tel. 21 44 695; April and Oct: daily 9am–park close; May-Sep: daily 9am–11pm; Nov-Christmas: daily 4–10pm*
This restaurant (formerly a bunker) changes its personality according to the season. In fine weather: a large terrace overlooking the Augarten Park and open-air concerts; in winter: mulled wine, pies and chestnuts around a bonfire in the courtyard. Entrées €6–8.

Aera (D A3)
→ *Gonzagagasse 11; Tel. 533 53 14; Mon-Sat 10am–1am; Sun 11am–midnight*
A neighborhood hangout with a warm, boisterous atmosphere, a huge bar and a bare decor of concrete floor, and recycled lamps. The food is an uninhibited mix of sweet and savory ingredients. Entrées €7.

Schöne Perle (D B2)
→ *Grosse Pfarrgasse 2 Tel. 0664 243 35 93; Daily noon (10am Sat-Sun)–11pm*
Spot the *funghetto* (an amazing Italian pinball machine) in the entrance. The spacious room with spartan decor serves up a healthy Austrian cuisine

with Mediterranean flavors, and vegetarian options: avocado and coriander salad, grilled calamari and potatoes with parsley, falafels, etc. Entrées €7–15.

Expedit (D C3)
→ *Wiesingerstrasse 6 Tel. 512 33 13 23 Mon-Fri noon–11pm; Sat 6pm–11pm; Sun 6pm–10pm*
An excellent restaurant offering cuisine from the Italian region of Liguria. The dining room is made of mostly large communal tables and high industrial shelving, remnants of the space's past life as a textile warehouse. Don't miss the homemade tagliatelle with chestnuts and truffle ravioli. Entrées €12–18.

Österreicher Im MAK (D C4)
→ *Stubenring 24 Tel. 714 0121; Daily 8.30am–1am (kitchen until 11.30pm)*
The wonderful airy, modern café-restaurant of the MAK Museum. Seasonal classic and modern Viennese cooking: crispy pike-perch in a walnut crust, calf's liver with asparagus. Vast garden terrace. Entrées €7–20.

Vincent (D B2)
→ *Grosse Pfarrgasse 7*

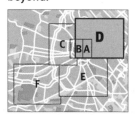

...CHLES **CAFÉ PRÜCKEL** **FAME SKATESHOP VIENNA**

Tel. 214 15 16
Mon-Sat 5.30pm–midnight
A cozy restaurant with black parquet floor, gorgeous red carpets, dark curtains and beautifully laid tables. The food is imaginative and just as elegant: lobster and black pudding ravioli, lamb with rosemary polenta. Discreet, attentive service. Entrées €20–35. Prix fixe (seven courses) €75.

Steirereck (D C4)
→ *Am Heumarkt 2a*
Tel. 713 31 68; Mon-Fri noon–2.30pm, 6.30–10pm
One of Vienna's most raved-about restaurants, with a romantic decor, a beautiful leafy terrace, comfortable armchairs, candles and views onto the Stadtpark. Reserve ahead. Entrées €35–40.

CAFÉS, BARS, CLUBS

Tachles (D B2)
→ *Karmeliterplatz 1*
Tel. 212 03 58; Mon-Fri 5pm–2am; Sun 6pm–1am
This bar on the pretty Karmeliterplatz is so convivial that customers feel free to linger over their beer for hours, while trying to figure out the collection of road signs or swaying to the sounds of the live music.

Café Prückel (D B4)
→ *Stubenring 24; Tel. 512 61 15; Daily 8.30am–10pm*
'The perfect place for people who want to be alone but who need company in order to do so' – is how the poet Alfred Polgar described the typical Viennese café. With its spacious rooms and warm atmosphere, it perfectly embodies the sentiment here.

Copa Cagrana (D F1)
→ *Donauinsel subway*
On either side of the New Danube are pavement cafés where you can be lulled by the gentle lapping of the water.

Urania (D C3)
→ *Urania; Tel. 713 33 71 Daily 9am–midnight*
A friendly café underneath an enormous glass roof, with great views over the Danube. In fine weather, the large terrace upstairs is a cozy place to relax.

Bricks (D C2)
→ *Taborstrasse 38; Tel. 216 37 01; Daily 8pm–4am*
A basement bar lounge with a dance floor and a 1970s mirror ball. Nicely mixed, easy listening music, and comfy nooks.

Flex (D A2)
→ *Donaukanal / Augartenbrücke Tel. 533 75 25; Daily 8pm–*

4am (6pm in summer)
The Vienna night spot on the banks of the Donaukanal. A mixed crowd gathers in the huge auditorium, which is the hub of the independent music scene. Electric atmosphere until dawn.

CONCERTS

Konzerthaus (D B4)
→ *Lothringerstrasse 20 Tel. 242 002*
A temple (1911) dedicated to classical music: four large auditoria, the most recent (2000) an ultramodern addition devoted to avant-garde creations. Its concert schedule is on a par with that of the nearby famous Musikvereinssaal (**E** D1).

Kursalon (D B4)
→ *Johannesgasse 33 Tel. 512 57 900*
The Salonorchester Alt Wien put on Mozart and Strauss concerts every evening, in the enchanting setting of a Viennese palace.

SHOPPING

Karmelitermarkt (D B2)
→ *Karmelitermarkt Mon-Sat 6am–7.30pm (5pm Sat)*
Surrounded by

magnificent façades, this pretty open-air market is always crowded. The stalls with their colored awnings are brimming with local produce: fruit, vegetables, fish, regional wines and cut flowers.

Porges (D B4)
→ *Weihburggasse 22 Tel. 513 19 35; Mon-Sat 10am–6pm (5pm Sat)*
A tiny fashion boutique run by a team of Dutch designers with great ideas. If you thought items like bolero jackets and frilly petticoats were out of fashion, think again! Very helpful staff.

Fame Skateshop Vienna (D B3)
→ *Franz-Josefs-Kai 31–33 Tel. 532 56 71; Mon-Sat 10.30am–6.30pm (5pm Sat)*
Everything imaginable for the skateboarder, this is also the outlet for the Fame brand.

Song Boutique (D C3)
→ *Landskrongasse 2 Tel. 532 28 58; Mon-Sat 10am–7pm (6pm Sat)*
Elegant, original outfits for all occasions: silk dresses and all types of fur coats to wear with multicolored bags and outlandish heels. An extensive selection that is easy on the eyes, though not always on the pocket.

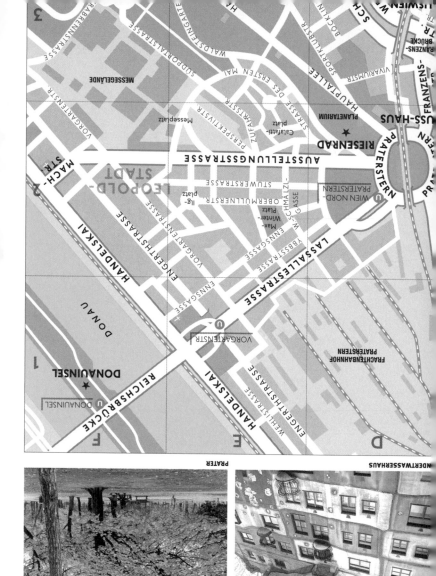

PRATER

HUNDERTWASSERHAUS

AUGARTEN

DONAUINSEL

otball matches, the
niature Lilliputbahn train
a place for a simple stroll
hong the chestnut trees.
Riesenrad (D D2)
Prater 90; Daily, May-Sep:
m– 11.45pm; March-April,
t: 10am–9.45pm;
v-Feb: 10am–7.45pm
e Giant (or Ferris) wheel,
Viennese landmark and
e dramatic background in
amous scene from Orson
elles' *The Third Man*
)49), has been gracefully
d slowly (allow 20
nutes for the ride) turning
ice 1897, when it was
ected to celebrate the
th anniversary of Franz-
seph's coronation. It

offers a splendid panorama
over the vast wooded Prater
and the rooftops of the
former imperial city.
★ Strauss-Haus (D C2)
→ *Praterstrasse 54*
Tel. 214 01 21; Tue-Sun 10am–
1pm, 2–6pm
The former home of Johann
Strauss Junior, 'the Waltz
King' (1825–99). This is
where he composed the
Blue Danube (1867), which
you can listen to among
other compositions as you
look around. Amusing
caricatures and many
original scores.
★ Wiener
Kriminalmuseum (D B2)
→ *Grosse Sperlgasse 24*

Tel. 214 46 78
Thu-Sun 10am–5pm
This pretty 17th-century
soap makers' house
illustrates the history of
murder in all its gory detail,
with medieval torture
instruments and chilling
modern photographs. The
tour ends on a less sinister
note in the pleasant
surroundings of the
courtyard.
★ Augarten (D B1)
→ *Park: daily 6.30am–dusk;*
guided tours of the porcelain
factory (tel. 211 24 18)
Mon-Fri at 10am
Vienna's first baroque
garden (1712), laid out by
the Frenchman Jean Tréhet:

hedge-lined paths, perfectly
symmetrical flower beds,
manicured lawns, and two
anti-aircraft defense towers
(*Flakturm*) that are sinister
reminders of World War 2.
The porcelain factory (1744)
is in the Gartenhaus.
★ Donauinsel (D F1)
'Spaghetti island' is a 13-
mile strip of land created by
the massive New Danube
development scheme
(1957–72), where pretty
boats bob up and down,
and a lighthouse shines its
beacon on the skyscrapers
of the nearby UN-City. A
good launching point for
watersports, and to the
south is a bird sanctuary.

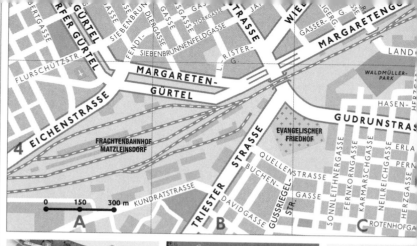

Map labels: WIEDNER GÜRTEL, MARGARETENGÜRTEL, WALDMÜLLER-PARK, MARGARETEN-GÜRTEL, EICHENSTRASSE, FLURSCHÜTZSTR., HASEN-, GUDRUNSTRASSE, EVANGELISCHER FRIEDHOF, FRACHTENBAHNHOF MATZLEINSDORF, QUELLENSTRASSE, TRIESTER STRASSE, BUCHEN-, GASSE, DAVIDGASSE, GUSSRIEGELSTR., KUNDRATSTRASSE, SONNLEITHNERGASSE, FERNKORNGASSE, KARMARSCHGASSE, NEILREICHGASSE, HERZGASSE, ROTENHOFGASSE, ERLA, PERN

0 150 300 m

4

A **B** **C**

SCHWARZENBERGPLATZ

BELVEDERE / UNTERES BELVEDERE

BELVEDERE / OBERES BELVEDE

★ **Secession Building (E** C1)
→ *Friedrichstrasse 12; Tel. 587 53 07; Tue-Sun 10am–6pm*
This dazzling gold-and-white symbol of the Secession Movement, designed by Josef Maria Olbrich (1898), was the first manifestation of the Jugendstil, which rejected the Historicist architecture of the Ring. The inscription on the frontispiece reads: 'To each era its art, to art its freedom'. The façade, embellished with an array of animals, is topped by an eye-catching golden dome. Inside, a dazzling frieze by Klimt pays tribute to Beethoven inside.

★ **Majolikahaus and Medallion House (E** B1)
→ *Linke Wienzeile 38–40*
Two wonderful houses designed by Otto Wagner, the genius of the Viennese Jugendstil. The façade of the Majolikahaus, entirely covered in tiles, is an explosion of pink and green ceramic floral designs. Gilded medallions depict female forms on the walls of the adjacent apartment block (1898).

★ **Gemäldegalerie der Akademie der bildenden Künste (E** C1)
→ *Schillerplatz 3; Tel. 588 160; Tue-Sun 10am–6pm*
The Academy of Fine Arts (1692) is housed in a neo-Renaissance (1876) building on the Ring. In the painting gallery are priceless works of art such as the triptych of the *Last Judgment* by Hieronymus Bosch, and a magnificent collection of Flemish and Dutch paintings, including *Portrait of a Young Woman* by Rembrandt and *Self-Portrait* by Van Dyck.

★ **Karlskirche (E** D1)
→ *Karlsplatz*
Mon-Sat 9am–12.30pm, 1–6pm; Sun noon–5.45pm
A baroque mix of classical and Byzantine architecture with Greek-style columns and minarets, the church of St Charles Borromeo, designed by Fischer von Erlach (1737), was built to glorify the Habsburgs, defenders of the Catholic faith. The dome is inspire by St Peter's in Rome and decorated with a fresco by Rottmayr depicting the fig against the Plague.

★ **Wien Museum Karlsplatz (E** D1)
→ *Karlsplatz; Tel. 505 87 47 Tue-Sun 10am–6pm*
Tracing the city's development from Roman times (1st century) when i was known as Vindobona there are fragments of the cathedral destroyed by

E

GEMÄLDEGALERIE DER AKADEMIE

SECESSION BUILDING

MAJOLIKAHAUS AND MEDALLIONS

Fertile ground for experimentation since the 18th century, Karlsplatz is an eclectic architectural mix, with the baroque Karlskirche, its famous concert halls and the Secession Building – manifesto of the eponymous movement. The nearby commercial Wienzeile has ornate façades in the same style, but Mariahilfer Strasse with its colorful crowds, gaudy window displays and futurist street lamps is more modern. On the slopes of the Belvedere, the majestic embassies stand aloof from the bustle of the city, while across the Gürtel, the pedestrian Favoriten Strasse leads to the splendid public baths of Amalienbad.

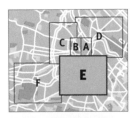

DOAN

AROMAT

RESTAURANTS

Doan (**E** C1)
→ *Naschmarkt 412; Tel. 585 82 53; Mon-Sat 7am–11pm*
In the heart of the buzzing Naschmarkt, this attractive stall offers cheap fresh, seasonal produce amid the banter of the market vendors. Delicious Greek-style breakfast. Entrées €5–12.

Hanil Sushi (**E** C1)
→ *Rechte Wienzeile 7 Tel. 585 35 90; Daily 11.30am–11pm (10pm Sun)*
'Running sushi' is the subtitle on the shop sign, and this is exactly what happens here, with a conveyor belt laden with Japanese and Korean specialties. Entrées €6–12.

Aromat (**E** C1)
→ *Margaretenstrasse 52 Tel. 913 24 53 Tue-Sun 5–11pm*
A friendly, informal restaurant behind an impressive Art Nouveau entrance, run by three young people who gave up their studies in favor of cooking. Imaginative daily-changing menu with many vegetarian options (soups, salads, crepes, galettes). Entrées €8–14.

Horvath (**E** B1)
→ *Hamburgerstrasse 2*
Tel. 585 73 00
Mon-Sat 8am–midnight;
Sun 10.30–3pm
This restaurant boasts inventive Austrian cuisine with international influences, using fresh produce from the neighboring Naschmarkt. Relaxed designer decor, spacious terrace and tiny recessed bar overlooking the Saturday flea market. Entrées €10–16.

Theatercafé (**E** C1)
→ *Linke Wienzeile 6 Tel. 588 30 405 Mon-Fri 3pm–midnight; Sat 10am–midnight*
Close to the Theater an der Wien, this big café frequented by theatergoers. Noisy discussions at the bar, a cozier atmosphere at the tables and a secluded back room in which to enjoy one of the house's cigars. Entrées €10–16.

Bodega Española (**E** D2)
→ *Belvederegasse 10 Tel. 504 55 00; Mon-Sat 4pm–midnight (6pm Sat)*
You will find mouthwatering tapas (try the cod with orange and olives) in this little corner of Spain close to the Belvedere. Andalusian decor and large open fire in winter. Entrées €8–27.

CAFÉS, ICE CREAM PARLOR

Café Sperl (E C1)
→ *Gumpendorfer Strasse 11*
Tel. 586 41 58; Mon-Sat 7am–11pm; Sun 11am–8pm (closed Sun July-Aug)
With creaky floorboards, delicate stucco, wood-paneled walls, embroidered banquettes and a pool table, the beautiful Sperl, opened in 1880, is still full of charm. Sit back and let yourself be lulled by the gentle drone of hushed conversation.

Café Phil (E C1)
→ *Gumpendorfer Strasse 10*
Tel. 581 04 89
Daily 9am (Mon 5pm)–1am
Once you hit the cozy couches here you might find it hard to get back on your feet, especially if you pick up one of the books scattered amongst the knickknacks. The laid-back, sometimes live, music only adds to the mood of indolence.

Rüdigerhof (E B1)
→ *Hamburgerstrasse 20*
Tel. 586 31 38
Daily 9am–2am
A vast, old-fashioned café opened in the early 1900s, with yellowed walls, tattered seating, threadbare carpets on the floor, and a lovely terrace overlooking the water in summer.

Tichy (E E4)
→ *Reumannplatz 13*
Tel. 604 44 46; Mid-March-Sep: daily 10am–11pm
This ice cream parlor is renowned for its wide choice of flavors and its Eismarillenknödel (ice cream dumplings with fruit preserves), sorbets and Italian delicacies.

BARS, CLUBS, CONCERTS

Nachtasyl (E A2)
→ *Stumpergasse 53*
Tel. 596 99 77
Daily 8pm–4am
A favorite of the Viennese and Eastern European bohemian set, the "night asylum" has posters on the walls and shabby tables for laid-back conversations that go long into the night. Regular concert (from 10pm) of music from Central Europe.

Transporter Bar (E C1)
→ *Margaretenstrasse 54*
Tue-Sat 7pm–2am (4am Thu-Sat)
The destination for the city's gay and alternative communities. Great cocktails, busy dance floor and live music at weekends, when the place is packed.

Mocca Lounge (E C1)
→ *Linke Wienzeile 4; Tel. 293 78 02; Daily 10am–2am*
This bar, warmly decorated in neo-colonial style, offers not only superb cocktails but also a great assortment of teas and coffees.

Ost-Klub (E D1)
→ *Schwindgasse 1*
Tel. 505 62 28; Mon-Sat 7pm–2am (4am Fri-Sat); July-Aug: Tue-Sat 10pm–4am (approximate schedule)
A wind from the Balkans blows through this club: concerts of Slav and Gypsy music, beer from Bohemia and dancing.

Musikverein (E D1)
→ *Bösendorferstrasse 12*
Tel. 505 81 90
Designed by Theophil von Hansen, the prestigious auditorium (1867), with its graceful gilded caryatids, is the venue for symphony concerts and the Vienna Philharmonic Orchestra's famous New Year concert. Standing €4–7.

SHOPPING

Naschmarkt (E B1)
→ *Wienzeile*
Mon-Sat 6am–6pm (9pm Sat); flea market: Sat 6.30am–6pm
This vast cosmopolitan market full of exotic and regional fare has been around since the 16th century. Fresh produce is on display in the neat little booths, while the ground is given over to the flea market and various knickknacks.

Opocensky (E D2)
→ *Favoriten Strasse 25*
Tel. 505 08 52
Tue-Fri 11am–9pm
A small gourmet deli with a selection of dishes that can be eaten on the spot.

Blumenkraft (E C1)
→ *Schleifmühlgasse 4*
Tel. 585 77 27; Mon-Fri 10am–7pm; Sat 9am–2pm
Exotic flowers on slender stems and transparent designer vases.

Le Miroir (E B2)
→ *Strobachgasse 2*
Tel. 0650 941 34 71; Tue-Fri 1–7:30pm; Sat 10am–6pm
A miniature two-story boutique filled with dresses in a wide range of fabrics and colors.

Design of 20th (E B2)
→ *Margaretenplatz 3*
Tel. 911 22 48
Mon-Fri 11am–7pm
Vases, laminate shelving and other nostalgic mementos of the 20th century in this fascinating second-hand store.

KARLSKIRCHE

WIEN MUSEUM KARLPLATZ

▲ Map D

D
DER
ÜNSTE   KÄRTNER   **SCHWARZENBERG-**
KÜNSTLER   RING   ★ **PLATZ**
HAUS   BÖSENDORFERSTR.
OTHRINGERSTRASSE   MUSIKVEREIN

E

F

ARLSPL.
Karlsplatz   ★ **WIEN MUSEUM**
HE   **KARLPLATZ**   ZAUNERGASSE
ÄT G
★
KARLSKIRCHE

AM HEUMARKT
SALESIANERGASSE
NEULING-
AM MODENA-PARK
STROH-
LINKE BAHNGASSE
RECHTE BAHNGASSE
REISNER-STRASSE
GASSE
GASSE

NEULINGGASSE

1

GARDEKIRCHE
SHAUSSTR.   RUSS-
SCHWINDG.   HELDEN-
WOHLLEBENG.   DENKMAL
PALAIS
SCHWARZENBERG

RENN-
METTERNICHG.
JAURÉSG.

DAPONTEG.
UNGAR-
LAND-
BARICHGASSE
JUCHGASSE

TECHNISCHE
UNIVERSITÄT

ARGENTINIERSTRASSE

HAUS
DES SPORTS

PRINZ

UNTERES
BELVEDERE

SALESIANER-
KLOSTER

WEG

KRANKENHAUS
RUDOLFSTIFT
✚

FUNKHAUS
TAUBST.

ARBEITER-
KAMMER

PLÖSSLG.

BELVEDERE-
GARTEN

BELVEDERE
★

BOTANISCHES
INSTITUT

MECHELG.

KLIMSCH-
SCHÜTZENGASSE

BOERHAAVEGASSE

RENN-

STRASSE

THERESIANUM

THERESIANUMGASSE

FAVORITENSTRASSE

EUGEN

GASSE

WIEDEN

BELVEDERE

GASSE

St.-Elisabeth-
Platz

VIKTOGASSE

GOLDEGGASSE

STRASSE

OBERES
BELVEDERE

BOTANISCHER
GARTEN DER
UNIVERSITÄT

JACQUINGASSE

FASANGASSE

GERLGASSE
HEGERGASSE
KÖLBLGASSE

HOHLWEGGASSE

MOHS-

GASSE

KHUNNG.

KLEIST-

GASSE

KARCHERG.

WEG

2

A.-BLAMAUER-GASSE

BESTATTUNGS-
MUSEUM

WEYRINGERGASSE

ALPEN-
GARTEN

ALAIS
NBURG-
ENSTEIN

HITZKY-G.
EINGASSE

Südtiroler
Platz
Ⓤ
SÜDTIROLER PLATZ

GÜRTEL

SCHWEIZER
SCHW.-GTN.-
STR.

ARSENALSTRASS

SÜDBAHNHOF

20ER HAUS

LANDSTRASSER

GÜRTEL

GARTEN

GHEGASTRASSE

KELSENSTR.

HEERESGESCHICHTLICHES
MUSEUM
★

3

IEDNER

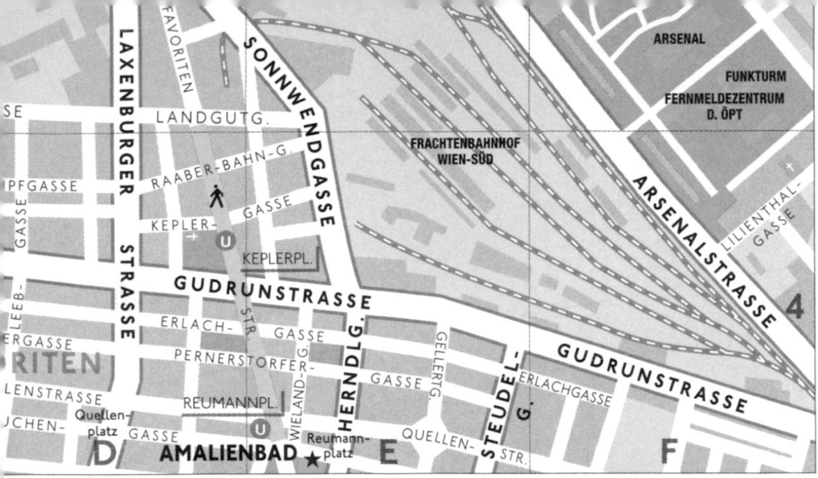

HEERESGESCHICHTLICHES MUSEUM **AMALIENBAD**

nbs, documents on the kish sieges, and works eading artists of the pos – Vienna's heyday.
Schwarzenbergplatz)1)

ing, perfectly nmetrical square rounded by charming ldings: the remarkable Nouveau-style French bassy (1903) as an standing example of endstil; the neo-baroque us der Kaufmannschaft amber of Commerce) h its globes borne in mph; and the fine oque Schwartzenberg ace (Hildebrandt and cher von Erlach). In the

square stands a memorial to the liberation of Vienna by the Red Army (1945).

★ **Belvedere** (E E2)
→ *Rennweg 6 / P. Eugen-Str. 27; Tel. 795 57 333*
Daily 10am–6pm
Ostentatiously designed by Hildebrandt, this was the summer home of the mighty Prince Eugene of Savoy.

★ **Unteres Belvedere**
The Lower Belvedere (1716) houses the Museum of Baroque Art with its rich collection of grimacing masks by Messerschmidt (1736–83). A magnificent climb up through the gardens leads to the Upper Belvedere.

★ **Oberes Belvedere**
As its name suggests, the palace (1722) commissioned by the Prince has unrivalled views. It has a magnificent wrought-iron gate, exquisite chapel, a vestibule with monumental Atlas figures and the Austrian 19th- and 20th-century gallery holding almost all of Klimt's work, as well as works by Schiele, Van Gogh and Renoir.

★ **Heeresgeschichtliches Museum** (E F3)
→ *Arsenal; Tel. 795 61*
Daily 9am–5pm
Inside the vast Byzantine-Moorish style arsenal (1856) is the fascinating Museum of Military History,

illustrating the conflicts of the Imperial armed forces and of Austria up until 1945. Enthusiasts will enjoy the Tank Garden.

★ **Amalienbad** (E E4)
→ *Reumannplatz 23; Tel. 607 47 47; Tue 9am–6pm; Wed, Fri 9am–9.30pm; Thu, Sun 7am–6pm; Sat 7am–8pm*
This outstanding example of Art Deco public baths was the flagship building of the Austromarxist city authorities (1919–34). Colorful mosaics in the lobby, wood paneling, ceramic tiles and wrought iron, with a curved glass roof over the swimming pool that floods it with light.

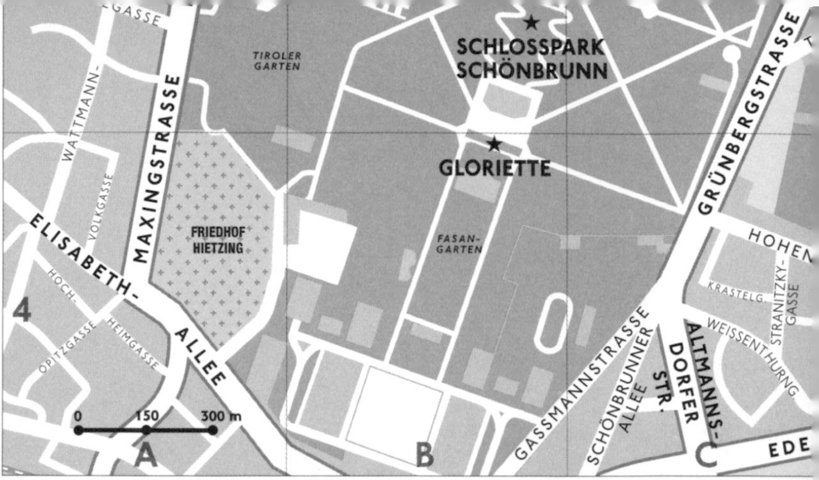

Map labels:
GASSE
TIROLER GARTEN
SCHLOSSPARK SCHÖNBRUNN ★
GLORIETTE ★
GRÜNBERGSTRASSE
WATTMANN-
MAXINGSTRASSE
VOLKGASSE
ELISABETH-
HOCH-
OPITZGASSE HEIMGASSE
FRIEDHOF HIETZING
ALLEE
FASAN-GARTEN
HOHEN
KRASTELZ-
STRANITZKY-GASSE
WEISSENTHURNG
SCHÖNBRUNNER ALLEE
GASSMANNSTRASSE
ALTMANNS-
DORFER STR.
EDE
4
0   150   300 m
A   B   C

HIETZING

AM PLATZ

★ Schloss Schönbrunn (F C3)
→ Tel. 811 130
Daily 8.30am–5pm (6pm July-Aug; 4.30pm Nov-March);
Imperial Tour (22 rooms);
Grand Tour (40 rooms)
Grandiose and awe-inspiring, this is the favorite residence of the Habsburgs, built from plans by Fischer von Erlach (1696) and modified by Nicolaus Pacassi (1749). Enter by way of the huge main courtyard (Ehrenhof) and come upon the majestic, ocher-colored, 1,441-room castle. The interior is a rococo extravaganza. Highlights include: the Great Gallery

with crystal mirrors and ceiling frescos by the Italian Guglielmi (1714–73); the Old Laquer Salon with lacquered wall panels and a marquetry floor; the Porcelain Room; and the Million Room covered in rosewood paneling inlaid with Mogul miniatures.

★ Schlosspark Schönbrunn (F B3)
→ Daily 6.30am to dusk
The principles of the French garden are applied to stunning effect in this hillside domain: straight rows of hedges rise skyward or plunge toward the city, the eye is drawn upward to the Gloriette or downward

to the castle. The Tyrolean and botanical gardens are worth a visit, as are the mock Roman ruins and the baroque section with its magnificent Neptune's Fountain (1780), the obelisk, and the statues of mythological creatures. There are stunning views over Vienna and the mountains of the Wienerwald to be seen from the top of the hill. At sunset, the yellow hue of the palace turns a deep, fiery ocher.

★ Gloriette (F B4)
→ Schlosspark Schönbrunn
The unmissable Gloriette (1775) sits in splendor on top of the hill. This

neoclassical triumphal a commemorates the victo of Maria-Theresa over th army of Frederick II of Prussia (1757), and is decorated with sculpted trophies and the Habsbu two-headed eagle. There are magnificent vie from the roof in summer.

★ Tiergarten (F B3)
→ Tel. 877 92 94; Daily 9am 6.30pm (4.30pm winter)
A natural history enthusi François III of Lorraine allowed Maria-Theresa to accede to the throne so t he could devote himself his passion – founding Europe's first zoo in 1752 The result is a set of eleg

F

SCHLOSS SCHÖNBRUNN

SCHLOSSPARK SCHÖNBRUNN

The tranquil summer residence of the Habsburgs, the splendid palace of the 'beautiful spring' (Schönbrunn) witnessed some of history's greatest events: the two eagles over the entrance bear testimony to Napoleon's stay here; it was at Schönbrunn that Charles I announced his abdication (1918); and it played host to the Kennedy-Khruschev summit in 1961. Nowadays, the public stroll casually through the rooms and around the magnificent park. There is still a pastoral atmosphere in the streets of neighboring Hietzing. On the hillside opposite, from the top of the lively Hutteldorfer Strasse, is a magnificent view of the Gloriette at Schönbrunn, a pale glow in the night sky.

MARIAHILFERBRÄU

CAFÉ GLORIETTE

RESTAURANTS

Kaiser Pavillon (F B3)
→ *Schlosspark Schönbrunn Tiergarten; Tel. 879 35 56 Daily 9am–4.30/6.30pm (variable)*
At the center of the zoo is this elegant octagonal 18th-century pavilion, a former observation building belonging to the imperial family. Now a restaurant, the mirrored interior has fine marquetry work and a large portrait of Franz-Joseph. Serving an 'imperial' breakfast, a wide range of soups and international cuisine. Entrées €6–14.

Mariahilferbräu (F E1)
→ *Mariahilfer Strasse 152 Tel. 897 47 49; Daily 8am (11am Sat-Sun)–midnight*
This large restaurant offers modest but excellent food. The decor is unashamedly kitsch, with exposed pipes on the high ceiling and a pulpit presiding over the floral motifs on the bar. This eccentricity is echoed in the somewhat old-fashioned soundtrack. Entrées €6–20.

Brandauer's Schlossbräu (F A2)
→ *Am Platz 5 / Hietzinger Hauptstr. 3; Tel. 879 59 70 Daily 10am–1am*

Set back from a little alleyway is a vast former baroque dance hall decorated with stucco, gilt and cherubs. Under the ceiling hung with banners, beer enthusiasts gather to enjoy their favorite brew and copious Austrian dishes. No less than nine draught beers. Entrées €7–15.

Gasthaus TirolerGarten (F B3)
→ *Schlosspark Schönbrunn, Tiroler Garten; Tel. 879 35 56 50; Daily 9am–10pm (6.30pm Oct-Feb)*
A spruce wooden chalet on the wooded slopes of the Tyrolean garden with a rustic decor, walls hung with ancient farm implements and engravings of the Alps. Specialties from Tyrol: try the famous *Tiroler Knödel* (meatballs with cabbage and cumin), with an Adam Bräu, the regional beer. Entrées €10–14.

Plachutta Hietzing (F A2)
→ *Auhofstrasse 1; Tel. 877 70 87; Mon-Fri 11.30am–2.30pm, 6.30–10.30pm; Sat-Sun 11.30am–10.30pm*
A cozy rustic restaurant in the quiet avenues of Hietzing. Seasonal dishes, Viennese cuisine, and meat hotpots, the

Street names, monuments and places to visit are listed alphabetically. They are followed by a map reference, of which the initial letter(s) in bold (**A, B, C**...) relate to the matching map(s) within this guide.

CAR

Cars should give absolute priority to pedestrians, bicycles and buses.

Speed limit
← 50 km/h (30mph) in cities; 100 km/h (60mph) outside built-up areas; 130 km/h (80mph) on freeways

Restricted parking
← Mon–Fri 9am–10pm
Parking is only allowed for two hours at a time. Parking disks available from kiosks.

Parking lots
← 24/7 (pay parking lots) Stephansplatz (A B3), Staatsoper (B D6), Rathaus (C C4), etc.

TRAIN AND COACH

Train stations

Westbahnhof (F F1)
Trains to northern France and northern Europe.

Südbahnhof (E E3)
Closed. To be replaced in 2012 by the nearby Wien Hauptbahnhof.

Bahnhof Meidling (F F4)
Substitute for Süd-bahnhof until 2012: trains to southern Europe.

Wien-Mitte (D C4)
Coaches to western Europe.

Reservations

Train (ÖBB)
← Tel. 517 17; oebb.at

Coach Eurolines (D D4)
← Tel. 798 29; Erdbergstrasse 202

TRAMWAY

Pension Riedl (A C3)
← Georg-Coch-platz 3
Tel. 512 79 19
www.pensionriedl.at
This homely hotel offers ten rooms, some with a view of Otto Wagner's post office. The owner takes pleasure in preparing outings or guided tours for her guests. €85–110.

Pension Schönbrunn (F D3)
← Schönbrunner Schlossstr. 30
Tel. 813 50 270
pension-schoenbrunn.at
Not far from the famous imperial castle is the fine blue-tiled and wrought-iron entrance of this hotel. The rooms are spacious and well equipped, with a view over the rear garden. €86–99.

Am Brillantengrund (C B5)
← Bandgasse 4
Tel. 523 3662
hotel-am-brillantengrund.at
Behind a pretty flower-covered façade is a large courtyard with a balcony around which the light-filled, impeccably neat rooms are arranged. In summer, the doors can be flung open and there's a swing for children. €85–156.

€100–220

Hotel Austria Wien (A C2)
← Fleischmarkt 20
Tel. 515 23
hotelaustria-wien.at
In the heart of Vienna, close to the Stephansdom. 46 rooms with tasteful, classical decoration. The numerous facilities include bike rentals, a copious breakfast, and a bar with an excellent selection of local wines. €109–175.

Landhaus Fuhrgassl-Huber (northeast of C A1)
← Rathstrasse 24
Tel. 440 30 33
Bus 35A to Neustift am Walde stops outside the hotel; fuhrgassl-huber.at
The capital seems a long way from this valley of the Wienerwald: a nearby pine forest and vineyards surround this comfortable inn, only 30 minutes from the Ring. From €115–138.

Hotel zur Wiener Staatsoper (A B5)
← Krugerstrasse 11
Tel. 513 12 74
zurwienerstaatsoper.at
Classical sculptures over a splendid wrought-iron doorway, gilt stucco, a magnificent tiled floor inside. This palatial hotel boasts double doors, double glazing, and crystal chandeliers. Attentive staff cater for guests' every need. €115–150.

Hotel Römischer Kaiser (A B5)
← Annagasse 16
Tel. 77 510
hotel-roemischer-kaiser.at
With its ornate, salmon-pink baroque stucco façade, the 'Roman emperor' hotel, in a sumptuous building dating back to 1684, is ideal for a luxury stay. €130–195.

Hotel Rathaus Wine & Design (C C4)
← Lange Gasse 13
Tel. 400 11 22
hotel-rathaus-wien.at
In a perfect location, this modern, stylishly hotel, owned by two oenophiles, is dedicated to wine. Large and comfortable rooms. Wine lounge; wine tastings and other events. €148–199. Breakfast €15.

Altstadt Vienna (C C5)
← Kirchengasse 41
Tel. 522 66 66; altstadt.at
A huge staircase with wrought-iron rails and contemporary works of art on the walls. The entire building is lavishly decorated: unique rooms.

STATIONS AND STOPS

leading off endless corridors, divans in all styles and a riot of color. €139–209.

Wandl (A A3)

→ Petersplatz 9; Tel. 534 55
hotel-wandl.com
Quiet and very central, this vast hotel is illuminated by two light wells. Top-quality, attentive service and two pleasant glass-roofed areas: the lobby at the front and the dining room. €170–220.

More than €220

König von Ungarn (A C3)

→ Schulerstrasse 10
Tel. 515 840; kvu.at
A bright yellow façade, vast sunlit patio, balconies with fine wood paneling and a modern bar under the medieval arches: this is a splendid 16th-century residence where the client is treated to world-class hospitality. From €220.

Astoria (A A5)

→ Führichg. 1; Tel. 515 770
austria-trend.at
A spacious reception room evocative of Vienna in the 1900s, with numerous examples of Jugendstil ornaments and liveried personnel. Long, wide corridors and rooms full of character. €220–450.

Das Triest (E C1)

→ Wiedner Haupstrasse 12
Tel. 589 18 80
dastriest.at
Huge gilded mirrors, giant beds, unusual use of space and monochrome walls: this is breathtaking design by Terence Conran at his very best. The amazing bar is reminiscent of a luxury train.
From €289.

LUXURY HOTELS

Sacher (B D5)

→ Philharmonikerstrasse 2-4
Tel. 514 56; sacher.com
Founded by the Sacher family in 1876, this legendary hotel opposite the Staatsoper used to be a stopping place for the European aristocracy on their way to Italy.
€265–420.

Hotel im Palais Schwarzenberg (E D1)

→ Schwarzenbergplatz 9
Reopening mid-2011 after renovation works
The beautiful baroque palace of Hildebrandt and Fischer von Erlach: deep tranquility in a green setting not far from the Ring. From €350.

Hotel Imperial (E D1)

→ Kärntner Ring 16
Tel. 501 10 333
hotelimperialvienna.com
With its massive façade overlooking the Ring, this is Vienna's oldest and most lavish hotel, inaugurated in 1873 by Emperor Franz Joseph I.
€439–789.

PUBLIC TRANSPORTATION

U-Bahn
Operates the Viennese subway, buses, and tramways.
→ Erdbergstrasse 202
Tel. 790 9100
Network maps
→ From all ticket outlets
€2.50
Very useful in order to use trams and buses.
Operating times
→ 5am–12.30am
Tickets
They can be bought at ticket offices (main subway stations), machines (cash and credit card), Tabak-trafiken and on board.
→ Ticket offices: Mon-Fri 6.30am–6.30pm
Single ticket
→ €1.80 (€2.20 on board)
Four-journey travelcard
→ €7.20 (transferable)
24- or 72-hr travelcard
→ €5.70 and €13.60
Eight-day travelcard
→ €28.20 (transferable, and you can choose the days)
Wien-Karte
→ €18.50; wienkarte.at
Valid 72 hrs. Also entitles holder to reduced entrance to Vienna's museums & monuments (brochure supplied).
Nachtlinien (night bus)
→ 12.30am–5am, every 30 mins; €1.80 (four journeys: €7.20)
22 routes departing from Schwedenplatz, Oper or Schottentor.
S-bahn
Tickets valid in zone 100 (central Vienna, to the main railway stations), special fares applicable beyond.

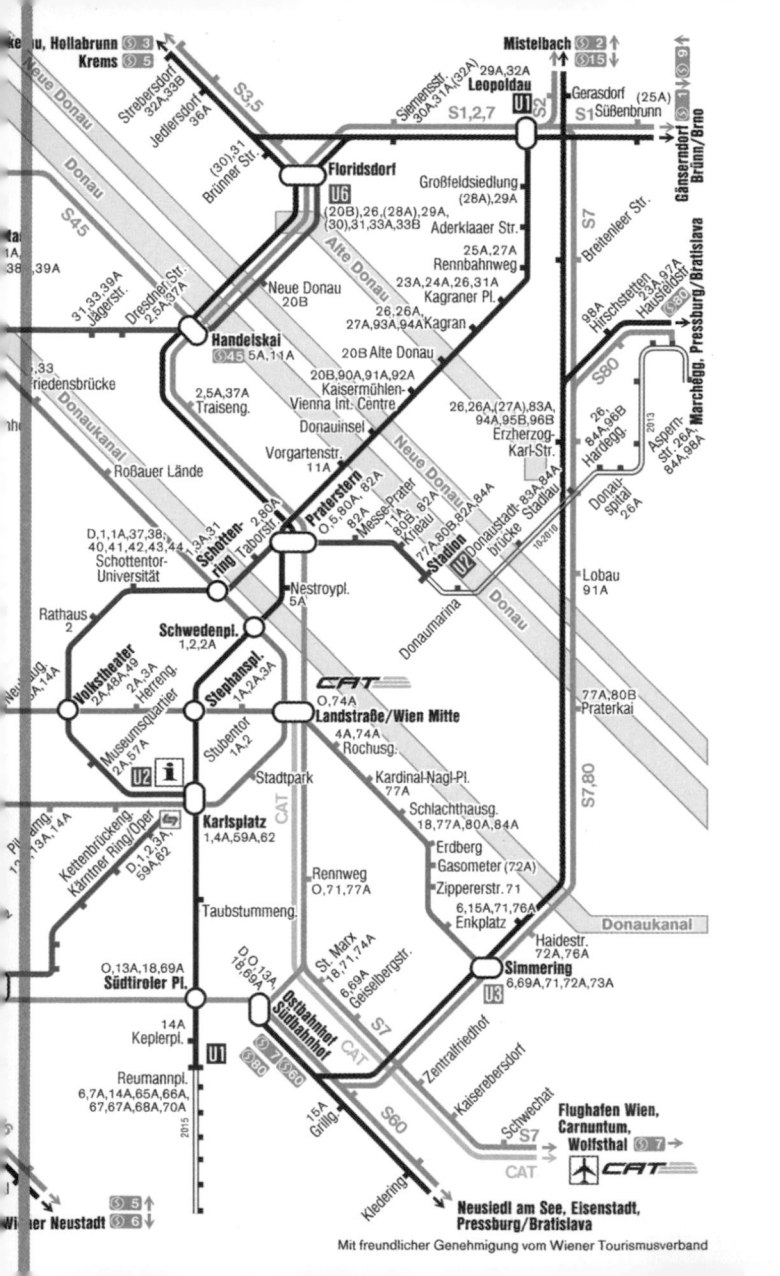

Mit freundlicher Genehmigung vom Wiener Tourismusverband

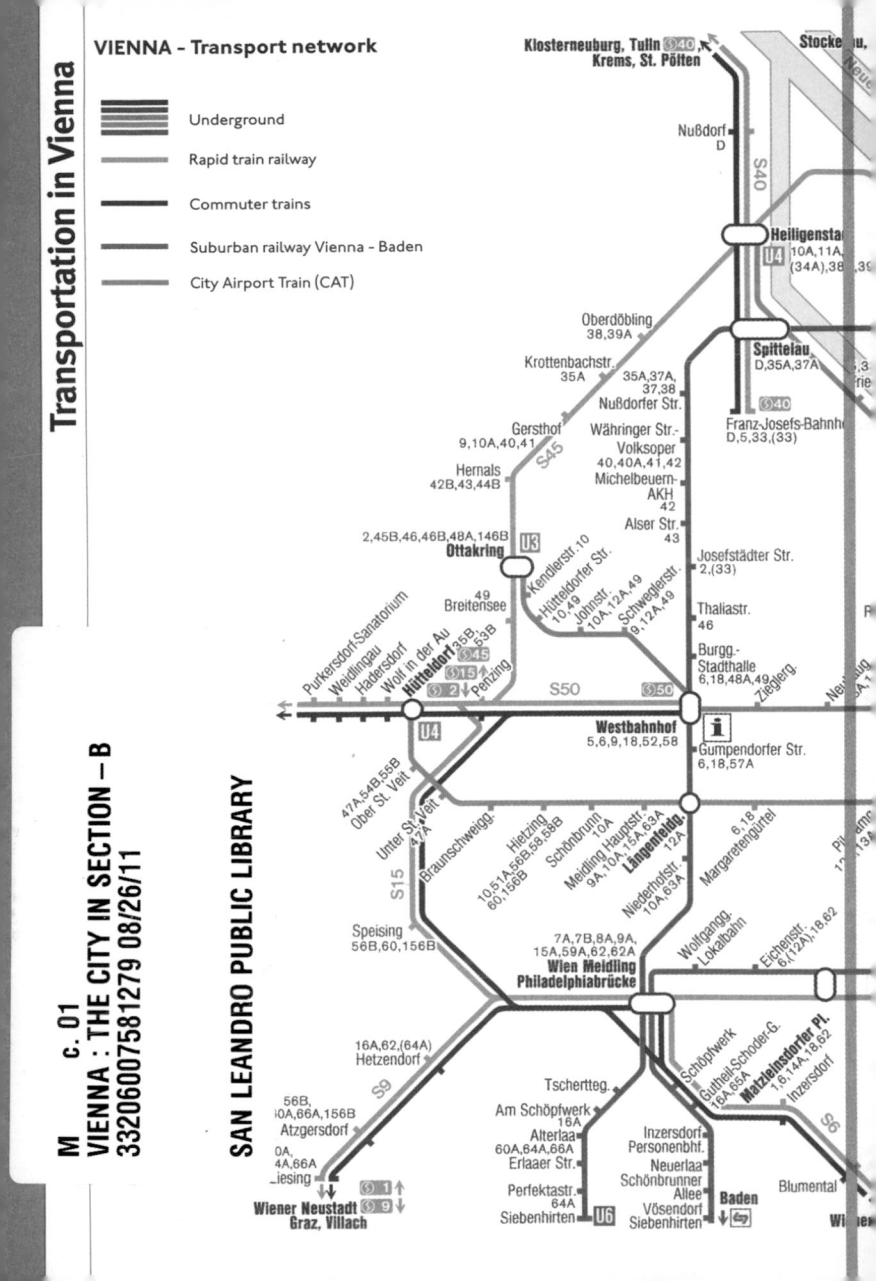

VIENNA - Transport network

Transportation in Vienna

Underground
Rapid train railway
Commuter trains
Suburban railway Vienna – Baden
City Airport Train (CAT)

Klosterneuburg, Tulln S40, Krems, St. Pölten

Stockerau,

Nußdorf D

S40

Heiligenstadt
U4 10A,11A,
(34A),38, 39

Oberdöbling
38,39A

Spittelau
D,35A,37A

Krottenbachstr.
35A

35A,37A,
37,38
Nußdorfer Str.

Franz-Josefs-Bahnhof
D,5,33,(33)

S40

Gersthof
9,10A,40,41

Währinger Str.-
Volksoper
40,40A,41,42
Michelbeuern-
AKH
42

S45

Hernals
42B,43,44B

Alser Str.
43

2,45B,46,46B,48A,146B
Ottakring   U3

Kendlerstr.10

Josefstädter Str.
2,(33)

49
Breitensee

Hütteldorfer Str.
10,49

Johnstr.
10A,12A,49

Schweglerst.
9,12A,49

Thaliastr.
46

Burgg.-
Stadthalle
6,18,48A,49
Zieglerg.

Purkersdorf-Sanatorium
Weidlingau
Hadersdorf
Wolf in der Au
Hütteldorf
S45
S15
9 2 Penzing

S50

S50

Westbahnhof
5,6,9,18,52,58

Gumpendorfer Str.
6,18,57A

U4

47A,54B,55B
Ober St. Veit
47A

Braunschweig.

Hietzing
10,51A,56B,58,58B
60,156B

Schönbrunn
10A

Meidling Hauptstr.
9A,10A,15A,63A

Niederhofst.
10A,63A

Längenfeld
12A

6,18
Margaretengürtel

S15

Speising
56B,60,156B

7A,7B,8A,9A,
15A,59A,62,62A
Wien Meidling
Philadelphiabrücke

Wolfgang-
Lokalbahn

Eichenstr.
6,12A,18,62

16A,62,(64A)
Hetzendorf

Schöpfwerk

Gutheil-Schoder-G.
16A,65A

Matzleinsdorfer Pl.
1,6,12A,18,62

Inzersdorf

S6

S9

Tschertteg.

56B,
60A,66A,156B
Atzgersdorf

Am Schöpfwerk
16A

0A,
4A,66A
Liesing   9 1

Alterlaa
60A,64A,66A
Erlaaer Str.

Perfektastr.
64A
Siebenhirten   U6

Inzersdorf
Personenbhf.

Neuerlaa
Schönbrunner
Allee
Vösendorf
Siebenhirten

Baden

Blumental

Wiener Neustadt   9 9
Graz, Villach

i

AIRPORT

Flughafen Wien-Schwechat
→ *viennaairport.com*
12½ miles SE of the Ring
To the city center
By bus
→ *To Morzinplatz (A B1) in 25 mins; daily 6.20am–12.20am, every 30 mins; €6; to Südbahnof-Westbahnof in 20–30 mins; daily 6am–midnight; every 20 mins; €6 (one way)*
By train (CAT) / subway
→ *To Wien-Mitte in 16 mins; daily 6am–11.30pm, every 30 mins; €10 (one way)*
→ *S-Bahn line S7 in 25 mins; daily 5am–midnight; €3.60*
By taxi
→ *Journey 25 mins; €35*

AIRPORT AND ROAD ACCESS

• *Unless specified otherwise, prices are for a double room en suite, breakfast included*
• *Hotels in the 1st district are much in demand and therefore expensive but there are many cheaper hotels in the outer districts (2nd to 9th), near the Ring. In the 1st district, the small pensions are recommended (reservation essential)*
• *Wherever you go, however, reservation is strongly advised in high season (June-Sep) and essential during the Christmas period*

FLAT RENTALS

Austrian National Tourist Office
→ *Tel. 0811 60 10 60*
austria.info
Contact the National Tourist Office to receive by fax or email a list of rooms and flats by district.
Pension Lerner (A C3)
→ *Schulerstrasse 18*

Tel. 533 52 19
pensionlerner.com
This boarding house also has three aparments full of old-fashioned charm (wallpaper with Biedermeier motifs, tall ceilings and parquet floors) behind the Stephansdom, so very central. Large reductions for long stays. €66–78.
Mondial Apartement Hotel (C C1)
→ *Alserbachstrasse/ Pfluggasse 1; Tel. 310 71 80*
mondial.at/apartment
Seven studios and nine spacious apartments decorated in typical Viennese style. All mod cons and close to the trams. Studio €95; breakfast €11.

YOUTH HOSTELS

The official Youth Hostels charge a small supplement for non-members (around

€3). Rooms and dormitories have safes.
Do Step Inn (F E1)
→ *Felberstrasse 20*
Tel. 982 33 14; dostepinn.at
It combines two options: a youth hostel for those on a tight budget and cozy hotel for others. €15–40/pers.
Hostel Ruthensteiner (F E1)
→ *Robert Hamerlingg. 24*
Tel. 893 4202
Open 24/7
hostelruthensteiner.com
A little wooden sign in a quiet street advertises this comfortable hostel. There are one to eight beds in each room, a kitchen area, a laundry and summer barbecue facilities in the courtyard. €16–38 per person. Breakfast €2.50.
Jugendherberge Myrthengasse (C B5)
→ *Myrthengasse 7*
Tel. 523 63 16; Open 24/7
oejhv.or.at

Ten minutes from Ring, in an elegant 19th-century building; a courtyard with creeping ivy and two-to six-bed dormitories (male and female separate, except groups). Numerous extras (games room, Internet, laundrette) and perfect cleanliness. €17.50/pers. (€21.50 non-members).
Hostel The Lounge (F E1)
→ *Mariahilfer Strasse 137*
Tel. 897 23 36
Open 24/7
wombats-hostels.com
A friendly hostel close to the Westbahnhof. Rooms with two to six beds, copious buffet breakfast, large lobby with games room and a bar in the basement. €18–29/pers.
Schlossherberge am Wilhelminenberg
(off map, east of C A3)
→ *Savoyenstrasse 2*
Tel. 485 85 03700; Bus 46B to the Ottakring subway

S-BAHN

station; hostel.at/shb
This hostel, surrounded by vineyards and pine woods on the slopes of the Wienerwald, is close to the luxurious Wilhelmberg castle. Well-kept rooms (one to four beds in each), and a pretty terrace overlooking the meadows. €19–60 per person.

Less than €100

Pension Baltic (C B4)
→ *Skodagasse 15*
Tel. 405 62 66
The charming, vast, old-fashioned rooms have uneven floorboards, ancient stoves and small paintings on the walls. The large shady courtyard is the biggest open space in the 8th district. Warm welcome. From €40–70; breakfast €5.

Pension Wild (C C4)
→ *Lange Gasse 10; Tel. 406 51 74; pension-wild.com*

Behind the bustling Ring, this comfortable family hotel in Josefstadt offers solace from all the activity. With carpets and big armchairs, it is spotlessly clean, with extensive facilities and attentive service. Gargantuan breakfast buffet. €53–97.

Altwienerhof (F E2)
→ *Herklotzgasse 6*
Tel. 892 60 00
altwienerhof.at
There is something of the grandiose in this hotel, with its colored marble decorations in the octagonal reception room. Elegant 'Altwiener' style tapestries on the walls and beautifully designed furniture. And there is a leafy courtyard in which to enjoy a peaceful breakfast. €70–107.

Pension Neuer Markt (A B4)
→ *Seilergasse 9*
Tel. 512 23 16;

hotelpension.at/neuermarkt
Ideally located at the heart of the Graben Stephansplatz-Kärtner Strasse 'golden triangle', in a building with a superb Jugendstil interior. Step out of the antique wooden elevator onto a red carpet leading to the quiet, immaculate rooms that look out onto the streets of the city center. Very friendly staff. €76–135.

Pension Andreas (C C3)
→ *Schlösselgasse 11*
Tel. 405 34 88
hotelpensionandreas.at
A delightful family-run boarding house in a quiet street right at the heart of the city center. The proprietor, Frau Seyeddain, has a fund of fascinating anecdotes about her small hotel, whose guests include 'theatricals' from the nearby Burgtheater. €77–110.

BOAT

For an excursion on the Danube or a trip on the Donaukanal.
DDSG Blue Danube
→ *Handelskai 265* (**D** E1)
Vorgartenstrasse subway station; Tel. 588 800;
ddsg-blue-danube.at
Departures daily (April-Oct), for the Wachau, Bratislava and Budapest.

TAXIS

Plentiful and inexpensive.
Fare
→ *Basic fare €2.50*
(€2.60 11pm–6am)
€1.20/km up to 4 kms
(€1.35/km), €0.90 after 4 kms (€1.05/km)
Reservations
→ *Tel. 313 00; 401 00; 601 60; 814 00*

BICYCLE

Riding
There are more than 620 miles of cycle lanes in Vienna and its suburbs.
CityBike scheme
→ *citybikewien.at*
There are 60 Citybike stations, open 24/7. Registration costs €1, the first hour is free, then you pay by €1/hour.
In the subway
→ *You can take your bike in the subway Mon-Fri 9am–3pm and from 6.30pm; Sat from 9am; Sun all day; special ticket €0.90*
Rental
Riebl Sport (E B2)
→ *Schönbrunner Str. 63*
Tel. 544 75 34
Mon-Fri 9am–6pm; Sat 9am–5pm (1pm summer); €12 per day

FPAVILLON

TECHNISCHES MUSEUM WIEN

roque pavilions, now
th modern fittings that
ow visitors to observe the
o inmates in comfort: Nile
codiles and Peruvian
nguins among a range
mammals, arachnids,
phibians, and insects.
Palmenhaus (F B3)
s is Europe's biggest
ss and metal tropical
enhouse (1882),
mprising 45,000 panes
glass. There are three
nate zones: tropical,
der the central dome
o century-old palm trees
ch the ceiling); mild,
nperate under the north

dome (plants from Asia
and New Zealand); and
humid, equatorial under
the south dome (luxuriant
vegetation).

★ **Hietzing (F** A3)
The most prestigious
district of Vienna, close
to Schönbrunn and the
Wienerwald, has numerous
Biedermeier and
Jugendstil houses. No. 48
Trauttmannsdorffgasse is a
house with a bas-relief
depicting a joyful putti
scene; no.50, the
Fürstenhof building (1905),
has a stunningly elegant
façade; no.21 Laroche-
gasse, the Villa Schopp,
has a delicate wrought-iron

entrance; no. 16, the Villa
Primavesi (1915), is an
example of classicism
revisited; and no. 29
Wattmanngasse is a
'gingerbread house' with
stunning majolica tiles.
★ **Hofpavillon (F** B2)
→ Schönbrunner Schloss Str.
Tel. 877 15 71
Visits by reservation
This unexpectedly lavish
subway station was
designed for the emperor
by Otto Wagner (1899).
The sumptuous octagonal
waiting room offers a bird's
eye view of Vienna.
★ **Am Platz (F** A2)
A lovely square, around
which stands a little white

church with a tall spire,
the local Hietzing Museum,
with extensive
documentation on Schiele,
and the yellow ocher Post
Office building (1770), the
former residence of Maria-
Theresa's ministers of
Foreign Affairs.
★ **Technisches
Museum Wien (F** C2)
→ Mariahilfer Str. 212
Tel. 899 98 6000
Daily 9am (10am Sat-
Sun)–6pm
The Technical Museum
(1908) is built around three
spacious, pretty courtyards
and has reopened its
collections (energy,
transportation, etc.).

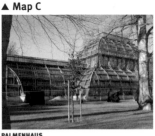

GRIETTE   TIERGARTEN   PALMENHAUS

▲ Map E

SARGFABRIK

RAIMUND THEATER

ROSA

Austrian specialty.
Entrées €17–24.

Vikerl's lokal (F E2)
→ *Würffelgasse 4*
Tel. 894 34 30; Tue-Sat 5pm–
midnight; Sun noon–5pm
A small restaurant with a
discreet façade, dark
wood paneling and soft
lighting, serving classic
Austrian dishes with a
modern edge. Reservation
essential. Entrées €12–20.

CAFÉS, ICE CREAM PARLOR

Café Gloriette (F B4)
→ *Schlosspark Schönbrunn*
Tel. 879 13 11; Daily 9am–
8pm (5pm winter)
With its majestic exterior,
grandiose interior and
coffered ceiling, the
Gloriette is another
favorite with visitors and
the Viennese alike. Under
the beady eyes of the
Habsburg eagles, a vast
choice of coffee, tea and
cake is offered. The
terrace, shaded by
centuries-old trees and
offering panoramic views
over the city, is especially
pleasant in summer.

Café Dommayer (F A2)
→ *Auhofstrasse 2*
Tel. 877 54 65; Daily 7am–
10pm; live music Sat 2–4pm
This venerable café,
opened in 1727, still

exudes enormous charm.
The Viennese revere this
place, its crystal
chandeliers, its little
bandstand and open-air
theater, and the lush
garden where elderly
patrons come to spend
the afternoon in summer.

Eissalon Garda (F E1)
→ *Mariahilfer Strasse 140*
Tel. 892 34 30; Daily 9am–
11.30pm (10pm in winter)
A gem of an ice cream
parlor owned by Adriano
Zanoni from Lake Garda.
The creamy Italian
concoction comes in no
less than 36 flavors, or
you can try the smoothies.

BARS, CLUBS

Die Sargfabrik (F B1)
→ *Goldschlagstrasse 169*
Tel. 988 98 111
Restaurant: Mon-Fri noon–
11pm; Sun 10am–4pm
A boldly designed
building dedicated to
artistic expression.
Concerts and cultural
events are sometimes
organized around a
swimming pool. Very
good restaurant on the
first floor for pre- or post-
theater dinners.

U4 (F E3)
→ *Schönbrunner Str. 222*
Tel. 815 83 07; Mon-Tue, Thu-
Sat 10pm (8pm Mon)–5am

Conny, the bouncer, is a
well-known local character
who will tell you all you
need to know about this
legendary club, as he is
also its owner. Two
basement dance floors;
rock (Fri), funky disco (Sat).

THEATERS

Schlosstheater (F C2)
→ *Schlosspark Schönbrunn*
Tel. 0664 11 11 600
Performances in July-Aug
Stunning baroque theater
(1747) decorated in ornate
gold and crimson.
Operettas are performed
here in July and August.

Raimund Theater (F F2)
→ *Wallgasse 18–20*
Tel. 588 85; Performances:
Mon-Sat 7.30pm; Sun 6pm
The former imperial
theater (1893) is now the
venue for major musicals.
Entirely renovated, it has
a 1,200-seat auditorium.

SHOPPING

Artiquarium Fuchs (F A2)
→ *Hietzinger Hauptst. 22*
Tel. 876 46 81
Mon-Fri 3–7pm
An enthusiastic couple
who scours the world in
search of new decorative
ideas has assembled a
motley array of objects
in this shop, including a

fine collection of Berger
oil lamps.

Wallner (F A2)
→ *Hietzinger Hauptst. 23*
Tel. 879 25 43; Mon-Sat
9am–6.30pm (4pm Sat)
A relaxing haven for
devotees of natural
products: organic food
and cosmetics, herbal
medicines and expert
advice.

Bundy Bundy (F A3)
→ *Maxingstrasse 4a*
Tel. 877 71 60; Mon 11am–
6.30pm; Tue-Sat 8.30am–
6pm (7pm Thu-Fri)
One of the eleven salons
belonging to the city's
most stylish hairdressing
chain. Reasonable prices.

**Vienna
Spezialitäten (F** E1)
→ *Mariahilfer Strasse 134*
Tel. 813 09 67; Mon-Fri
10am–noon, 1–6pm;
Sat 10am–3pm
Collectors assemble in
this cheerful bazaar to
buy and exchange
stamps, coins, banknotes,
medals and even
effigies of Mozart.

Rosa (F E3)
→ *Meidlinger*
Hauptstrasse 134
Tel. 813 09 08; Mon-Sat
10am–7pm (6pm Sat)
A vast range of stylish
footwear at accessible
prices, from flashy
pumps to elegant boots.